The Journal of the History of Philosophy Monograph Series
Edited by Richard A. Watson and Charles M. Young

Also in this series

Epistemology and Skepticism: An Enquiry into the Nature of Epistemology

George Chatalian

Foreword by Roderick M. Chisholm

Published for
The Journal of the History of Philosophy, Inc.

SOUTHERN ILLINOIS UNIVERSITY PRESS
Carbondale and Edwardsville

Library of Congress Cataloging-in-Publication Data

Chatalian, George, 1920–
Epistemology and skepticism: an enquiry into the nature of
epistemology / George Chatalian; foreword by Roderick M. Chisholm.
p.   cm. — (The Journal of the history of philosophy monograph
series)
"Published for the Journal of the History of Philosophy, Inc."
Includes bibliographical references and index.
1. Knowledge, Theory of.   2. Skepticism.   3. Analysis (Philosophy)
I. Title.   II. Series.
BD161.C428   1991
121—dc20   90-38855
                                                                          CIP
ISBN 0-8093-1672-2

The paper used in this publication meets the minimum requirements of
American National Standard for Information Sciences—Permanence of
Paper for Printed Library Materials, ANSI Z39.48-1984. ∞

For Shirley Lenox Chatalian
without whom not

CONTENTS

THE *JOURNAL OF THE HISTORY OF PHILOSOPHY*
Monograph Series

THE *JOURNAL OF THE HISTORY OF PHILOSOPHY* MONOGRAPH SERIES, CONSIST-
ing of volumes averaging 80 to 120 pages, accommodates serious studies in the
history of philosophy that are between article length and standard book size.
Editors of learned journals have usually been able to publish such studies only
by truncating them or by publishing them in sections. In this series, the *Journal
of the History of Philosophy* presents, in volumes published by Southern Illinois
University Press, such works in their entirety.

The historical range of the *Journal of the History of Philosophy* Monograph
Series is the same as that of the *Journal* itself—from ancient Greek philosophy to
the twentieth century. The series includes extended studies on given philosophers,
ideas, and concepts; analyses of texts and controversies; new translations and
commentaries on them; and new documentary findings about various thinkers
and events in the history of philosophy.

The editors of the Monograph Series, the directors of the *Journal of the History
of Philosophy,* and other qualified scholars evaluate submitted manuscripts.

We believe that a series of studies of this size and format fulfills a genuine
need of scholars in the history of philosophy.

Richard A. Watson
Charles M. Young
—Editors

FOREWORD
Roderick M. Chisholm

DURING THE PAST TWENTY-FIVE YEARS THERE HAS BEEN A RENAISSANCE IN epistemology, or the philosophical theory of knowledge. It may well be that during this time more progress has been made with respect to the details of the subject than has been made at any comparable period during its history. Epistemologists have also been concerned with the nature of epistemology and with its relations to science, to the other areas of philosophy, and to our daily life. (To be sure, some have rejected the traditional questions and then, unfortunately, have described quite different questions as constituting the subject matter of epistemology.) Of the many works on the nature of epistemology that have appeared during this period, the present book seems to me one of the most profound and illuminating. It is a contribution of the first importance to the theory of knowledge, both systematically and historically.

Dr. Chatalian is concerned to show the inadequacy of what he calls the "new" conception of epistemology and to provide us with an account of the subject that is more nearly adequate to what epistemologists have been doing for the past 2,500 years. (An indication of his philosophical perspective is the fact that he uses "new" to refer to a conception which, as he says, came to be generally accepted during the first decade of the present century.)

He distinguishes a number of theses that typify this new, twentieth-century conception of epistemology. He is concerned to show that each of these is either unfounded or false.

He denies the most fundamental of these theses—that epistemology "is to be defined and otherwise explained in terms of skepticism." He argues that this thesis, as it is understood by those who defend it, is based upon two quite different misunderstandings—one pertaining to the nature of epistemology and the other to the nature of skepticism as an actual phenomenon in the history of philosophy.

Most of us, as Chatalian says, are "limited skeptics," but we may not agree about where the limits are to be drawn. The things that you are skeptical about may be quite different from the things that I am skeptical about. This kind of selectivity is especially striking in the case of those who are latitudinarian in assessing the justification of their own beliefs. Different theists may appeal to different ostensible sources of divine revelation; and when this happens, each is likely to be tough-minded with respect to the claims of the other.

It is a mistake to suppose that philosophers may be divided into skeptics and nonskeptics in the way in which, say, they may be divided into theists and nontheists. Consider the following observation made in the present book:

> Wittgenstein and Ayer deal with philosophical skepticism without dealing with their own skepticism with respect to the philosophical, the metaphysical, and the ethical; and Quine's very definition of skepticism in terms of sense perception rules out the very possibility and so the consideration of other forms, some of which (e.g., skepticism with respect to induction and the religious) are his own.

Chatalian throws new light upon the history of skepticism in Western philosophy. If what he says about Sextus Empiricus and Pyrrho is right, as it seems to me to be, then much of what has been written about these philosophers is mistaken; my own writings on the subject are no exception. And the current English translations should be revised in certain key respects. Sextus Empiricus, according to Chatalian's interpretation, was in no sense a general skeptic; he does *not* question the possibility of knowledge or of attaining the truth. What he questions is, rather, the possibility of knowledge about *philosophy* and about *science*. It is with respect to philosophy and science and not with respect to matters of ordinary life that suspense-of-judgment is to be recommended. Chatalian draws this general conclusion: "In the case of Sextus (the only supposed skeptic for whom there is a mass of primary data) there is overwhelming reason to believe that he is not a general skeptic, and . . . in the case of all the rest there is woefully insufficient reason to believe that any of them is."

The deeper source of our interest in epistemology, according to Chatalian, is simply the nature of man: "the natural tendency of the human mind to wonder about, to inquire into, and to reflect upon the questions whether it knows, how it knows, how much it can in principle know, and what it is to know at all."

Where Sextus Empiricus, according to Chatalian's interpretation, was skeptical about the possibility of scientific knowledge but not about the possibility of our ordinary knowledge, many contemporary philosophers seem to think that there is an impressive amount of scientific knowledge but that no one in particular knows anything. It is not redundant to add, therefore, that the deeper interest in knowledge to which Chatalian refers is a part of the Socratic concern to know ourselves.

PREFACE

THE PRESENT WORK HAD ITS ORIGIN IN A FEW PAGES OF ROUGH AND INFORMAL "Notes on Epistemology," which in late 1978 I distributed to my students in a senior course in epistemology at the University of Ife in Nigeria. By early 1983 those notes had become an extended paper which I submitted for publication in the journal *Philosophy and Phenomenological Research*. The paper was accepted provided that I make a number of changes suggested by the referee and endorsed by the editor. Among those changes were that its length be shortened and that its scope—too narrowly focused on one epistemologist—be widened. Its scope was extended, but so was its length, which by 1986 was double that of the original paper and approximately that of the present work. During those three years—largely devoted to a critical study, requested by the editor of another American journal of philosophy, of the worldview of an American philosopher recently deceased—the few sentences in the 1983 version concerned with Sextus Empiricus and Pyrrho became the fifty manuscript pages of the present work's sections 2.1 and 2.2 on the major Greek Skeptics, Sophists, and Plato; for by this time, back in the United States, I had access to primary materials unavailable in Nigeria and had decided to reexamine the whole question of the existence of general skeptics.

Notwithstanding the work's publication in the *Journal of the History of Philosophy* Monograph Series, I view it essentially as a philosophical, not a historical, study. The historical and linguistic investigations in it, important as they are, are decidedly secondary, undertaken because the philosophical outlook I take fundamental issue with—the analytic conception of epistemology and of philosophy—itself depends upon historical and linguistic hypotheses.

I am indebted to a number of persons to whom I gladly acknowledge my debt: first, to the editors of the Monograph Series (Richard A. Watson on the side of modern philosophy and Charles M. Young on the side of classical), whose numerous suggestions, both constructive and critical, substantially improved the final draft; to Dan Gunter, the copyeditor, whose numerous stylistic and other suggestions contributed to the improvement; to Scott Bowen, an old schoolfriend who went out of his way to obtain primary materials and much else for me at a time when I was unable to obtain them for myself; to the anonymous referee of *Philosophy and Phenomenological Research*, whose critical suggestions intentionally succeeded in broadening the scope of the work and unintentionally succeeded in lengthening it; to Hao Wang, who raised searching questions I have not addressed and have only just begun to face; and finally, and above all, to Roderick M. Chisholm, whose initial response in 1984 quietly encouraged me to continue when I might otherwise have given up, and without whom this work would never have seen the light.

1

The Problem: A General Introduction

1.1 A New Conception of Epistemology: Seven Theses

1.1.1 A NEW CONCEPTION OF EPISTEMOLOGY HAS ARISEN IN WESTERN PHILOSO-
phy since the turn of the century and has become increasingly widespread since
then: the conception that epistemology is to be defined and otherwise explained
in terms of philosophical skepticism.[1] The conception has been advanced and
propounded by a large number of writers in a number of theses taking a variety
of forms: (1) definitional (a definition of epistemology itself), (2) definitional
again (a definition of knowledge), (3) genetic (a thesis about the conditions under
which epistemology and all its problems arise), (4) semantic (a thesis about a
necessary condition of a question's making sense), (5) historical (theses about
the founder of epistemology and the period of its founding), (6) scopic (a thesis
about the scope of epistemology), and (7) existential (a thesis about the existence
of general skeptics). As the conception seems to have originated with Bertrand
Russell early in the century, it seems fair to identify it for convenient reference
as the Russellian conception, although over the course of the subsequent three-
quarters of a century elements—introduced by G. E. Moore, L. Wittgenstein,
and others—not to be found explicitly in the Russellian original have been
incorporated in the conception, modifying it in various ways.

1.1.2 Throughout his philosophical career Russell consistently defined epistemology and philosophy indistinguishably in terms of philosophical skepticism or
doubt:

> The essential characteristic of philosophy, which makes it a study distinct from
> science, is *criticism* . . . . Descartes' "methodical doubt," with which modern philos-
> ophy began . . . is rather the kind of criticism which we are asserting to be the essence
> of philosophy. . . . This is the kind of criticism which constitutes philosophy.[2]

More definitely:

> The definition of "philosophy" will vary according to the philosophy we adopt; all
> that we can say to begin with is that there are certain problems, which certain people
> find interesting, and which do not, at least at present, belong to any of the special
> sciences. These problems are all such as to raise doubts concerning what commonly
> passes for knowledge; and if the doubts are to be answered, it can only be by means
> of a special study, to which we give the name "philosophy."[3]

A. J. Ayer is one of a long line of post-Russellian philosophers who have
adopted the Russellian conception:

> In this book I begin by taking the question of what is meant by knowledge as an
> example of philosophical enquiry. Having maintained that to say that one knows a
> fact is to claim the right to be sure of it, I show how such claims may be disputed
> on philosophical grounds. Though their targets vary, these sceptical challenges
> follow a consistent pattern: the same line of reasoning is used to impugn our
> knowledge of the external world, or of the past, or of the experiences of others. The
> attempt to meet these objections supplies the main subject matter for what is called
> the theory of knowledge.[4]

D. W. Hamlyn, another in the post-Russellian line, has presented the conception
more comprehensively than has anyone else, has developed its ramifications
systematically, and has introduced Wittgensteinian and Popperian elements into
it. His adoption of the Russellian conception is not immediately apparent, however, for on the face of it he defines epistemology in seemingly traditional and
radically un-Russellian and un-Wittgensteinian terms: "Epistemology, or the
theory of knowledge, is that branch of philosophy which is concerned with the
nature and scope of knowledge, its presuppositions and basis, and the general
reliability of claims to knowledge."[5] In this case appearance and reality do not
correspond, however, as we shall see in chapter 2; the reality—his adherence to
the Russellian outlook—emerges when he characterizes the theory of knowledge
("epistemology" in our usage) and its problems in certain ways:

> In a certain sense . . . all the problems of the theory of knowledge, even the more
> general ones, arise against and by contrast with a quite different point of view. That
> is that knowledge is impossible, or at least that we can never be sure that we have
> attained it. This thesis, which may take a variety of forms, is known as philosophical
> skepticism. It raises fundamental doubts about the possibility of knowing anything
> at all.[6]

Here he characterizes all the problems of what he calls "the theory of knowledge";
elsewhere he characterizes just one of them: "When a philosopher asks whether
something is possible, the question must be set against the consideration that
this thing may not be possible. It must be set against a general skepticism

concerning the matter in question. To be called upon to justify the possibility of knowledge or of certain kinds of knowledge makes sense only on the supposition that it or they may not be possible" ("Epistemology," 9). In a third passage he characterizes epistemology ("theory of knowledge" in the first passage) itself:

> It is no coincidence that epistemology began in the context of a form of the Sophists' general skepticism about knowledge, for until such doubts had been raised, the possibility was bound to be taken for granted. . . . This general skepticism led to the beginning of epistemology as it has been traditionally known. . . . It was Plato . . . who can be said to be the real originator of epistemology, for he attempted to deal with the basic questions: What is knowledge? Where is knowledge generally found, and how much of what we think we ordinarily know is really knowledge? Do the senses provide knowledge? Can reason provide knowledge? What is the relation between knowledge and true belief? ("Epistemology," 9)[7]

This third passage mingles what I called above the historical thesis (thesis 5: about the originator of epistemology and about the period during which he originated it) and the genetic thesis (thesis 3: about the conditions under which epistemology and all its problems arise). The first passage mingles the genetic ("arises against") and the semantic ("by contrast with"); the second is a more explicit formulation of the semantic thesis (thesis 4: a thesis about a necessary condition of a question's making sense).

1.1.3 Although to the best of my knowledge no other writers subscribe to the semantic thesis, many do subscribe to one or another of the remaining six theses laid out above. Among the many philosophers subscribing to the genetic thesis is W. V. Quine:

> Doubt prompts the theory of knowledge, yes; but knowledge, also, was what prompted the doubt. Scepticism is an offshoot of science. The basis for scepticism is the awareness of illusion, the discovery that we must not always believe our eyes. Scepticism battens on mirages, on seemingly bent sticks in water, on rainbows, on after-images, double images, dreams. But in what sense are these illusions? In the sense that they seem to be material objects which they in fact are not. Illusions are illusions only relative to a prior acceptance of genuine bodies with which to contrast them. . . .
>   Rudimentary physical science, that is, common sense about bodies, is thus needed as a springboard for scepticism. . . . The sceptic's example of the seemingly bent stick . . . and his examples of mirages, after-images, dreams, and the rest are similarly parasitic upon positive science, however primitive.[8]

Another is John L. Pollock, who answers the question, "What is an epistemological problem?" as follows:

> Skeptical arguments generate epistemological problems. Apparently reasonable assumptions lead to the conclusion that knowledge of a certain sort (e.g., knowledge

of the physical world, or knowledge of other minds) is impossible. Faced with such an argument, our task is to explain how knowledge is possible. The problem is not to show *that* knowledge is possible; that much we can take for granted. What we must do is find the hole in the skeptical argument that makes it possible to have the knowledge we do. The problems of epistemology are problems of how we can possibly know certain kinds of things that we claim to know or customarily think we know. In general, given a statement P, we can ask, "How do you know that P?" This is the general form of an epistemological problem. The question "How do you know that P?" is a challenge—a demand for justification. The task of the epistemologist is to explain how it is possible for us to know that P, i.e., to explain what justifies us in believing the things we do.[9]

Similar accounts of the genesis of epistemology and more generally of philosophy are to be found among early members of the Vienna Circle—for example, Moritz Schlick and Hans Hahn—and in Bertrand Russell.[10]

1.1.4 Among the many who subscribe to one or both of the two parts of the historical thesis (the identification of the originator of epistemology as Plato, and the identification of the period of its origination as that of the *Theaetetus*) is W. K. C. Guthrie:

We see [he writes, during a discussion of Plato's *Charmides*] the first stirrings of the intellectual curiosity which led him later on, in the *Theaetetus* and *Sophist*, to look for the essence of knowledge itself, its relation to sensation and opinion, the possibility of error and related questions. He will found epistemology, but not yet. . . .

Now for the first time [he writes, in a discussion of Plato's *Theaetetus*] Plato has chosen to make knowledge itself the main subject of enquiry, setting aside for the purpose all preconceived ideas such as appear unchallenged in the *Phaedo-Republic* group.[11]

Others subscribing to this view are John Burnet, Bertrand Russell, and Nicholas P. White.[12]

1.1.5 I have so far summarily explained and documented theses 1, 3, 4, and 5. In section 1.3 I explain and document thesis 6, the scopic thesis, and in section 1.4 I explain and document thesis 7, the existence thesis. The remaining theoretical thesis—thesis 2, which concerns the conception of knowledge—I explain, document, and critically assess in section 2.3 on the basis of my assessments of thesis 7 in section 2.1 and thesis 5 in section 2.2.[13] In section 1.2, which forms an interlude, I determine and explain the broader philosophical foundations of the new conception of epistemology. I then advance an alternative conception of epistemology, and underlying it an alternative conception of philosophy, mainly in chapter 3, but partly also as part of my criticisms in chapter 2.

1.2 The New Conception of Epistemology
and Analytic Conceptions of Philosophy

1.2.1 This new conception of epistemology, unprecedented in the global history of philosophy, appears to be rooted in the new conceptions of philosophy, themselves unprecedented,[14] which, like the new conception of epistemology, were inaugurated by Russell early in the century, developed by Moore in certain directions, stated in their most extreme forms by members of the positivistic and linguistic movements in philosophy, and hailed as a revolutionary turning point in philosophy.[15] It was thus that Russell, arguing that the problems and methods of philosophy were misconceived by all the traditional schools of philosophy (whence come the widespread references in the "new" philosophy to "traditional philosophy," "traditional logic," "traditional metaphysics," "traditional ethics," "traditional epistemology," and so on, and the general redivision of philosophy in terms of "philosophy of science, . . . logic, . . . mathematics, . . . language, . . . government, . . . religion, . . . history, . . . art," and so on), advanced what he called the "logical-analytic" method in philosophy, redefined (thus reconceiving) philosophy as the science of the possible (making "only such assertions as would be equally true however the actual world were constructed"), reconceived all philosophical problems, "when subjected to the necessary analysis and purification, " as logical problems, and excluded all the rest of the traditional problems from the scope of general philosophy, which from now on was to be "scientific." In other words of his, logic is the essence of philosophy, and philosophy and logic are indistinguishable (elsewhere it was philosophy and epistemology, as I have already noted) "as ['logic'] has now come to be used."[16]

1.2.2 Post-Russellian philosophers more or less deeply influenced by Russell (much earlier by Hume, somewhat earlier by Moore, and later by Wittgenstein) then proceeded to substitute "analytic" or "conceptual" or "linguistic" for Russell's "logical," thus providing analytic-philosophical variants (Wittgenstein, Carnap, Ayer, Ryle, Waismann, Strawson, et al.) of Russell's logical-analytic original that have been espoused in various forms by various adherents of analytic philosophy: every philosophical problem, "when subjected to the necessary analysis and purification," is analytic, or conceptual, or linguistic; and its solution— for philosophical problems could now be solved, now that they were scientific— is analytic, or conceptual, or linguistic.[17]

By Wittgenstein, philosophy—whose 2,500-year-long classical tradition was repudiated by him as mostly nonsensical (largely, it appears, in ignorance of it)— was reconceived first as critique of language, then as investigation of the workings of our language;[18] by Rudolf Carnap, after a similar wholesale repudiation (on a similar basis), first as logical analysis of science (more technically, the logical syntax of the language of science), then as logical syntax supplemented by semantics, still later as logical syntax and semantics supplemented by pragmatics (in a series of works, including numerous books and papers, extending from the 1920s to the 1960s), always, however as philosophy of science (a view implicit in Wittgenstein, explicit in Quine);[19] by A. J. Ayer as the provision of contextual definitions;[20] by Gilbert Ryle as the systematic restatement of what it really means to say so-and-so, along with the detection of the linguistic sources of recurrent misconstructions and absurd theories, all the examples of which were to be found in the classical world tradition of philosophy;[21] by Friedrich Waismann, following Wittgenstein's lead, as the clarification of thought;[22] and so on.[23]

1.2.3 These reductionistic reconceptions of philosophy in general were followed in rapid succession by reductionistic reconceptions of every branch of classical or traditional philosophy: either the total repudiation of ethics as a legitimate part of the philosophical (or indeed of any cognitive) enterprise[24] or its reductionistic reconception in exclusively metaethical terms;[25] either the total repudiation of metaphysics as a legitimate part of any philosophical or cognitive enterprise[26] or its reductionistic reconception in exclusively meta-metaphysical terms, differing, as Strawson put it, from what is called philosophical, logical, or conceptual analysis only in scope and generality;[27] either the total repudiation of epistemology as a legitimate part of any philosophical or other cognitive enterprise[28] or its reductionistic reconception in exclusively metaepistemological terms;[29] and either the total exclusion of the applicational dimensions—political philosophy, social philosophy, economic philosophy—of the classical world tradition ("matters," as Russell wrote, "which I should regard as lying wholly outside philosophy")[30] or their reconception in exclusively linguistic terms.[31]

1.2.4 Meantime, both before and after Russell's earliest moves toward analytic philosophy, Moore introduced two other ideas—one methodological, the other doctrinal—which were eventually incorporated in the analytic conception of philosophy: the first, a switch in focus from the answers of philosophy to the questions, with the methodological requirement that the questions be subjected to prior analysis, "discovering precisely what *question* it is which you desire to answer"; and the second, the view that the propositions of common sense have priority over the propositions of philosophical theory, the truth of the former being unquestionable, and only their analysis being a matter for philosophical investigation.[32]

1.2.5 If we put some of these pieces together, we can understand how the generic account of the analytic conception of epistemology (allowing for variations or differences within the genus) was arrived at. According to Wittgenstein and the logical positivists, the only truths are those of natural science, the only method of discovering them is the method of science, and philosophy's sole positive function is not to discover or even to seek truths inaccessible to science and scientific method but only to analyze scientific truth and method: an exclusively second-order enterprise, eschewing all direct contact with and investigation of reality and human aspiration. According to Moore, the propositions of common sense (which, when it is common sense about physical bodies, Quine identifies with rudimentary physical science) must be added to the stock of scientific truths; and where those propositions, at least, are concerned, a major function of philosophy in that branch of it known as epistemology must be to erect what Hamlyn has characterized as a set of defense works against general skepticism.[33] And according to Wittgenstein, the advancement of all philosophical theory is out of bounds: philosophical problems—which are not empirical problems to be solved with the help of empirical data but linguistic problems to be solved or resolved by looking into the workings of our language—are not to be solved by discovering new information.[34]

If this is true for philosophy in general, it is necessarily true for all its branches. Thus, philosophy of mind neither requires nor provides any new information about minds; it merely rectifies the logical geography of the knowledge we already possess and have obtained solely through science and common sense.[35] Thus, the metaphysician does not and cannot discover any truths, new or old, about reality; he merely analyzes the actual structure of our thought about the world.[36] Thus, the moral philosopher does not and cannot discover any moral or ethical truths; he merely analyzes the propositions and terms of moral and ethical judgment.[37] And so it is for the epistemologist.

In his study of Wittgenstein, Anthony Kenny puts forward a conception of epistemology that is a widespread variant of the analytic conception: "Since the time of Descartes epistemology, or theory of knowledge, has been one of the major preoccupations of philosophy: the attempt to explain how it is that we know what we know, and how to answer sceptical doubts about the justification of our beliefs."[38] It is a definition framed in light of an analytic conception of philosophy (reproducing elements of the account given, e.g., by Russell, Ayer, Hamlyn, and Pollock): that we already know what it is that we know; that what we know is obtainable only by nonphilosophical and nonepistemological means; that philosophical and epistemological inquiry are in principle incapable of discovering any truth about reality and human aspiration; and that epistemology in particular has two and only two essential functions—the negative one being defensive (how to repel sceptical doubts or to erect a set of defense works against philosophical skepticism), the positive one being explanatory (explaining *how* it is that we know *what* it is that we know).

Arthur Danto has formulated the analytic epistemological outlook more plainly: "Philosophy, in providing theories of truth or theories of knowledge, . . . adds nothing to the body of truths which we possess or knowledge which we have. Only science, broadly construed, of course, does this. Philosophy only analyzes what it is for a sentence to be true, or what it is for a man to have knowledge."[39] But this, I shall argue, is not what epistemologists since the time of Descartes, or for that matter since the time of Plato and even before, have viewed as their whole task; it is only what epistemologists, when they have reduced epistemology to analytic epistemology, have viewed as their whole task.

1.3 Thesis 6: The New Conception of Epistemology and the New Conception of the Scope of Epistemology

1.3.1 The reductionist and exclusionist conceptions of philosophy advanced by analytic philosophers, issuing as they have in reductionist and exclusionist conceptions of epistemology (as of every branch of classical philosophy), have issued inevitably in reductionist and exclusionist conceptions of the scope of epistemology (as of every branch of classical philosophy). Just as Russell's logicalist or possibilist conception of philosophy excludes, by his own account, "many of the traditional problems of philosophy," and Wittgenstein's critical conception excludes, by his own account, "most of the propositions and questions to be found in philosophical works" (to say nothing of what his linguistic conception excludes), and Carnap's analytic conception, by his own account, "all of the traditional problems of philosophy," so the analytic conceptions of epistemology exclude most of the traditional problems and questions of epistemology. This is the case even when, as in the case of Hamlyn, the definition of epistemology advanced is, on the face of it, highly traditional and appears to take in all the problems of traditional epistemology.

1.3.2 In general, twentieth-century epistemologists, when they address these questions at all (Quine, for example, being one who does not), accept something like Hume's twofold division of philosophical skepticism into "excessive" (the Pyrrhonian, according to him) and "mitigated." Hamlyn distinguishes between "general" or "wholesale" skepticism and limited or restricted skepticisms—skepticism with respect either to special fields of knowledge (e.g., science, mathematics, and history) or to the means of knowledge (e.g., perception, reason, and memory). Ayer, ignoring the general or wholesale forms of skepticism, addresses himself exclusively to restricted or limited forms—skepticism with respect to our knowledge of physical objects, the past, induction, scientific entities, and other minds. Pollock, not ignoring general skepticism but repudiating it ("The problem is not to show *that* knowledge is possible; that much we can take for granted"), also addresses himself exclusively to the limited forms—skepticism with respect to our knowledge of the physical world, the past, contingent general truths, other minds, the a priori, "and possibly knowledge of general moral truths."[40]

1.3.3 Two striking features of these and many other accounts and critiques of limited skepticism are worth noting. The first is the arbitrariness of their selectiveness: there is no consideration or, for the most part, even any mention of limited philosophical skepticisms of other kinds—skepticism with respect to the philosophical itself, the ethical, the metaphysical, the epistemological, the religious, and the theological. If epistemology is in part a set of defense works against philosophical skepticism, it is not for Hamlyn or Ayer or Wittgenstein or Quine a set of defense works against all possible or even known forms of limited skepticism. Wittgenstein and Ayer deal with philosophical skepticism without dealing with their own skepticism with respect to the philosophical, the metaphysical, and the ethical; and Quine's very definition of skepticism in terms of sense perception rules out the very possibility and so the consideration of other forms, some of which (e.g., skepticism with respect to induction and the religious) are his own. It may indeed be the case that such limited forms of skepticism are justifiable; it is not at this point being argued that they are not. All that at this point is being argued is that they require justification: a general or adequate epistemology is not licensed to ignore them or to take it for granted that they are justifiable.[41]

The second feature worth noting fits in with a feature of analytic epistemology earlier noted: that the forms of philosophical skepticism against which defense works must be erected are those and only those which in the judgment of the analytic epistemologists undermine science and common sense (which, in Quine's scheme, is just to say science). One or the other of these two silent assumptions of analytic epistemology is traceable to Russell, Moore, Wittgenstein, Carnap, Ayer, and the early analytic epistemologists in general. Every dimension of classical or traditional philosophy is to be jettisoned except for the analytic, conceptual, or linguistic investigation and defense of science and common sense; and so I argue in section 2.3 that the reduction of the scope of classical epistemology in the new epistemology is even more drastic than I have so far remarked. If philosophy in the Middle Ages was viewed by many as the handmaiden of theology, philosophy and epistemology in the twentieth century have come to be viewed by the analytic philosophers and others as the handmaiden of science and common sense. Danto says so in so many words, and Ayer implies it.[42]

1.4 Thesis 7: Skeptics and Skeptics: General Skeptics and Limited Skeptics

1.4.1 If epistemology is in part or in whole a response to general skepticism, there must be general skeptics to whom to respond. But who are they, and just exactly what does their skepticism amount to? Many of the most noted critics of skepticism do not say; and many of those who say, say or imply what is not so.

Examples can be cited from the distant past and in the recent present. Hume, in the distant past, claims that he has very carefully displayed "the arguments of that fantastic sect" (the Pyrrhonian) whose adherents, according to him, "hold that all is uncertain, and that our judgment is not in *any* thing possest of *any* measures of truth and falsehood."[43] What—like so many of his twentieth-century descendants—he does not inform the reader is that his knowledge of that fantastic sect was secondhand, derived from Bayle's *Dictionary* and Montaigne's philosophical works, both of which misinterpreted Pyrrhonism.[44] His careful display of the arguments of that fantastic sect was a careful display (as I shall argue by implication in section 2.1) of a sect that never existed, and so, to use his own words, "Whoever has taken the pains to refute the cavils of this *total* scepticism, has really disputed without an antagonist." Ayer, in the recent present, maintains that not all philosophers are skeptics,[45] evidently viewing himself as one of those for whom that negated generalization is true (a view which in any case follows from his conception of epistemology).

But it is not the case that not all philosophers are skeptics. What *is* the case is that no philosophers are *general* skeptics (at least in the ancient world), and that all philosophers are *limited* skeptics. The idea that there is a special class of philosophers who are skeptics—for example, the Greek Sophists and the so-called Greek Skeptics of ancient Greece, all the rest not being so—cannot be sustained; and the whole history of philosophy has been distorted by the idea, along with all philosophical investigations of philosophical skepticism.

1.4.2 Myles Burnyeat, a noted student of the Greek Sophists, the Greek Skeptics, and skepticism generally, has in general terms severely criticized the uncontrolled license with which modern philosophers deal with skepticism:

> Skepticism is one of the few subjects which every philosopher thinks he knows a good deal about. The skeptical arguments in the classic texts of Descartes and Hume are so familiar a part of a philosophical education that every philosopher has given some consideration to the radical challenge to our knowledge of the world which these arguments present.
>
> Equally familiar is the way in which the modern philosopher feels free to construct skeptical arguments of his own and to describe them as "what the skeptic says," without worrying whether any historical skeptic did make himself vulnerable to the crushing refutation which then follows.[46]

In fact, the situation is far worse than even Burnyeat makes it out to be. Wittgenstein, Ayer, Ryle, Quine, and numerous others advance general characterizations of skepticism, skeptics, and skeptical arguments—as if they were not in fact dealing with straw men—without ever taking the trouble (witness Hume) to cite actual texts, skeptics, skeptical theses, or skeptical arguments justifying those characterizations.[47] With respect to all these contemporaries and many of their twentieth-century predecessors it is just as Burnyeat says it is: for Wittgenstein it is "Scepticism"—undefined, unexplained, uninstanced—which is "not irrefutable but obviously nonsensical, when it tries to raise doubts where no questions can be asked"; for Ayer always "the sceptic"—never identified, quoted, distinguished (as if they were all alike), or analyzed—who says this, that, or the other; for Ryle "thinkers"—never identified, and so on—"who wish to maintain the pre-eminence of mathematical knowledge over other beliefs, and . . . who wish to depreciate mundane beliefs in favour of supra-mundane beliefs"; and for Quine "doubt"— no doubter in particular ever being cited or the specific content of his doubt ever being explained—that prompts the theory of knowledge.

1.4.3 None of this would matter very much—although the question of responsible philosophizing cannot be evaded—if these critics gave a correct or reasonably adequate account of skepticism anyway; but in fact they do not, even when, unlike Wittgenstein, they give an account of it at all. There is no evidence—and Ryle cites none—that any of the ancient Greek Sophists or Skeptics wished to maintain the preeminence of mathematical knowledge over other beliefs or to depreciate the mundane in favor of the supramundane. There is no evidence— and Quine cites none—that the ancient Greek Sophists or Skeptics argued for general skepticism on the basis of sensory or perceptual illusion, and no evidence (or very little) that they argued for general skepticism at all (cf. section 2.1).

In his critical review of Strawson's *Introduction to Logical Theory*, Quine writes: "The anonymity of [Strawson's] 'formal logicians say' engenders an air of Strawson v. Strawman. The discipline of documenting his adversary might also have operated now and again as a corrective by leading him to wonder whether formal logicians do think quite the way he supposed they did, on certain points, after all."[48] And so it might. But the anonymity of Quine's— and Wittgenstein's, Ayer's, Ryle's, and Hume's—"doubt," "scepticism," "the sceptic," "what the skeptic says," and "one of those sceptics, who hold" engenders no less an air of Strawson v. Strawman; and the discipline of documenting the adversary might have operated now and again (or most of the time) as a corrective by leading them to wonder whether "skeptics" do think quite (or even remotely) the way their critics suppose they do, on most points, after all. The skepticism of Sextus Empiricus, for example, has a far narrower scope and a far wider basis than these critics of general skepticism think: it is not about all possible forms of knowledge, and it appeals to considerations far exceeding that of Quine's sensory illusion—for example, the argument from infinite regress, the argument from equipollence, the argument from the unresolvability of philosophical controversy, and the argument from the diallelus, not one of which is touched by Quine's abrupt critique of skepticism. Given the failure of these critics to grasp and to come to grips with the depth and breadth of what Chisholm has called "the problem of skepticism" and characterized as "one of the basic problems of the theory of knowledge and one which may well be incapable of solution,"[49] we must acknowledge the failure of their critical responses to that problem.

1.4.4 Among proponents of the new epistemology there is one who has taken the trouble to document the skeptical adversary. In four very substantial works, Hamlyn presents a general conception of philosophical skepticism; divides it into two species consisting of general skepticism and limited skepticism; defines both; distinguishes five different versions of the general and five different species of the limited; identifies two schools of general skeptics (the Greek Sophists and the Greek Skeptics); identifies a good many of their individual members; and cites texts in justification of his account.[50]

For Hamlyn, as for many of the proponents of the new epistemology, it is the existence of general skeptics and their general skepticism in response to which epistemology as a philosophical discipline has arisen and in terms of which it can be explained and even defined. According to him, the five different versions of general skepticism may be formulated as follows: first, that knowledge is impossible; second, that we can never be sure that we have attained it; third, that it makes no sense to speak of knowledge; fourth, that we never know anything; and fifth, that the possibility of knowledge is questionable.[51] I therefore turn now to the question of the existence of general skeptics.

2

Examination of Some Theses of the New Epistemology

2.1 Thesis 7: The Existence of General Skeptics

2.1.1 THE PRIME EXHIBITS. AMONG SPECIALISTS IN ANCIENT PHILOSOPHICAL skepticism and among epistemologists who have addressed themselves to the question, it is generally agreed that the prime exhibits among ancient skeptics are the Greek Sophists and the Greek Skeptics.[1] Others, however, are sometimes cited: Democritus, Metrodorus of Chios, Leucippus, and Xenophanes.[2] I deal with these in achronological order, starting with the Greek Skeptics, and starting first with the last of them.

2.1.2 *Sextus Empiricus.*[3] I advance a general thesis and ten subordinate theses with respect to Sextus. The general thesis is that he is not a general skeptic in any of the five senses specified by Hamlyn or in any other unarbitrary sense. The subordinate theses are as follows: first, he never explicitly asserts general skepticism; second, he never implies it by what he does assert; third, he never addresses himself to the general question of the possibility of knowledge or the attainability of truth; fourth, he addresses himself exclusively to the limited question of the possibility of knowledge or the attainability of truth in the fields of (what in his day were called) philosophy (*philosophia*), science (*epistemē*), and art (*technē*); fifth, he takes for granted throughout the possibility of knowledge or the attainability of truth with respect to many matters; sixth, he asserts at many points not only the possibility but also the actuality of knowledge and truth, categorically advancing numerous knowledge- and/or truth-claims; seventh, the suspense-of-judgment (*epochē*) whose necessity he argues for is a suspense-of-judgment solely with respect to philosophical, scientific, or artistic questions and hypotheses; eighth, the "nonassertion" (*aphasia*), even "speechlessness," of the Sextonian and Pyrrhonian Skeptic is not what so many have said it is—"refusal to say 'Yes' or 'No' about anything," "silence," or "speechlessness"[4]—and not even what Sextus himself says without qualification that it is—refusal to "affirm or deny anything"(P.i.9)—but only a refusal for the time being and under the circumstances to affirm or deny any of those philosophical, scientific, or technical doctrines; ninth, Sextus affirms thousands of propositions (without, of course, contradicting the Skeptic doctrine of *aphasia*) in the course of his two works; and tenth, all apparent instances to the contrary—one of which I have just quoted— can be seen to be only apparent and not genuine when his subsequent explanations are taken into full account.[5]

The total body of evidence relevant to these eleven theses is not only massive (only a small fraction of which has been taken into account by any student of skepticism) but Janus-faced: much of it appears to support and confirm them; but much of it appears to contradict and to falsify them.

2.1.2.1 *The supporting evidence.* Throughout his two works and at every critical juncture Sextus provides clear indications that the scope of his inquiry is limited. In the first eight books of those two works (the three of *Outlines* and the first five of *Mathematicians*) he makes it clear that what he will discuss is philosophical doctrine; and in the course of those eight books he examines all of the major and many of the minor philosophers in the history of Greek philosophy from Thales to the Stoics through the end of the pre-Christian era. At the very outset (chapter 1, "Concerning the Main Differences among the Philosophies"), making the first of the innumerable assertions of the sort that he as one of the Greek Skeptics is supposed by so many twentieth-century students to have eschewed, he distinguishes three possible natural results of any investigation of *any* object (discovery of it, denial of its discoverability, and persistence in the as yet unsuccessful investigation); three possible results of the investigation of *the objects of philosophy* (truth-claims about them, denial of the discoverability of the truth about them, and persistence in the investigation); the three main types of philosophy (the Dogmatic, which claims discovery; the Academic, which denies discoverability; and the Skeptic, which, explicitly repudiating both, persists in the investigation); the three main types of philosopher (the Dogmatist, e.g., the Milesian and Ionian *phusikoi,* the Platonists, Aristotelians, and Stoics; the Academic, e.g., Cleitomachus and Carneades; and the Skeptic, e.g., Pyrrho and Sextus); and the three main divisions of philosophy (Logic, Physics, and Ethics, corresponding roughly to what in modern philosophy is known as epistemology, metaphysics, and ethics [P.i.1–4; P.ii.13]).[6]

It is clear from all this that, so far, Sextus is not even addressing the general question of the possibility of knowledge or of the attainability of truth; he is addressing the limited question of the possibility of knowledge or the attainability of truth in philosophy. Even with respect to that limited sphere, he makes it clear that he is not asserting the impossibility of philosophical knowledge or the unattainability of philosophical truth. Such an assertion would be incompatible with the three further terms he adopts to characterize the Skeptic (which itself, in his day and in his usage, meant "Inquirer")—"Zetetic," "Ephectic," and "Aporetic" (P.i.7, at which his explanations may be consulted). Nowhere in his two works can he be found affirming any of Hamlyn's five formulations of general skepticism; and, that being the case, students are forced to "interpret" what he does affirm in terms of general skepticism.

This delimitation of the scope of his inquiry (an inquiry that itself is incompatible with general skepticism)[7] is indicated again and again: in book 2 of *Outlines* (P.ii.1; P.ii.12), where he says that he will discuss the several divisions of philosophy; in the same book (P.ii.1–259), where he discusses the logical division of philosophy (cf. P.iii.1); in book 3 (P.iii.1–167), where he discusses the physical division; and in the same book (P.iii.168–279), where he discusses the ethical division (cf. P.ii.13). The whole of volume 2 of the Loeb Classical Library edition is then devoted to logic (in two books), and the whole of volume 3 is divided between physics (in two books) and ethics (in the remainder of the volume). The whole of volume 4 is then devoted to the supposed sciences of grammar (book 1), rhetoric (book 2), geometry (book 3), mathematics (book 4), astronomy (book 5), and music (book 6). Nowhere in all this is there any critical investigation of the ordinary claims to knowledge and truth which are universally made in ordinary life, which Sextus himself makes as a matter of course, and which he everywhere sanctions and nowhere questions.[8]

In book 2 of *Outlines,* where the critical discussion of logic is first introduced (P.ii.1; P.ii.13), Sextus says that since the subject matter of all three divisions of philosophy requires testing and so a criterion (P.ii.13), he will begin with the doctrine of the criterion of truth (P.ii.4). But although that is what he says, it is clear both from the general context of his entire corpus and also from the particular contexts at various critical junctures that his inquiry is concerned not with the criterion of truth in general but with the criterion of philosophical (or scientific or technical) truth in general; for it is, apart from what he actually says, in fact the latter and the latter alone which he then proceeds to subject to critical discussion.[9] Distinguishing three senses of the term *criterion*—the general (e.g., physical organs, applicable to every standard of apprehension), the special (e.g., rule and compass, applicable to every technical standard of apprehension), and the most special (applicable to every technical standard of apprehension "of a non-evident [*adelon*] object")—he makes it clear that his critical discussion is to be confined to the third—that is, to "only logical standards and those which the Dogmatists employ for judging of truth" (P.ii.14–16). But since we already know that the notion of truth (according to Sextus) employed by the Dogmatists is the notion not of truth in general but of philosophical truth in general, we know that when Sextus asks, "Does a criterion of truth exist?" (P.ii.18), he is asking, elliptically, whether a criterion of philosophical truth exists. So when he thereupon advances the famous Wheel (*diallelus*) Argument—that "in order to decide the dispute which has arisen about the criterion [of truth], we must possess an accepted criterion by which we shall be able to decide the dispute; and in order to possess an accepted criterion, the dispute about the criterion must first be decided" (P.ii.20)—we know that the argument is designed to justify suspense-of-judgment (*epochē*) about claims to philosophical truth and not to justify general skepticism, as so many students have concluded.[10]

When, after his initial consideration of the question of the criterion of truth Sextus returns to it to devote a deeper and more sustained consideration to it (L.i.27), he prefaces his reconsideration by observing that the search for philosophical truth presupposes trustworthy principles and methods for the discernment of such truth and that it is the logical division of philosophy which seeks to provide the necessary theory of criteria and of proof (L.i.24). And why, he asks, is "the problem of this criterion . . . everywhere a subject of controversy"? Because, he answers, man is by nature a truth-loving animal (a most emphatic affirmation, we note) and because the criterion pronounces judgment upon the most general systems of philosophy concerning the weightiest of matters (L.i.27). Never can he be found affirming that knowledge of the existence of men, or of philosophers, or of philosophical systems, or of proposed criteria of truth, and on and on, is impossible; or that we can never be sure that we have attained it; or that it makes no sense to speak of knowledge of it; or that we never know anything about them; or that the possibility of knowledge of any of them is questionable. He takes it for granted that all are knowable, and in fact known. Since he time and again clearly restricts the subject of his discussion, he like any other writer is under no obligation to say endlessly, every time he poses a question and addresses possible answers, that the subject under discussion is restricted. It is the student's obligation to interpret what Sextus says at one point or another in terms of the general context and in light of the explanations provided.

Sextus conveys the delimitation of the scope of his inquiry in other terms: in terms of the distinction between the evident (*prodelon*) and the nonevident (*adelon*), when he explains that the Skeptic assents to nothing nonevident (P.i.13), thereby implying that the Skeptic assents to the evident; again in terms of the distinction between dogmatizing and not dogmatizing, when he explains that the Pyrrhonian philosopher (whose existence he evidently takes for granted) does not dogmatize, "using 'dogma' in the sense . . . of 'assent to one of the non-evident objects of scientific (*epistēmas*) inquiry' " (P.i.13), thereby implying that the Pyrrhonian philosopher gives or can give assent to evident objects; again the terms of the distinction between phenomena (*phainomena*) and the "external underlying things" (*ton exothen upokeimenon*), when he says that the Skeptic can justifiably say what appears to himself although he cannot justifiably say what if any the external underlying things (*substrata*, in Aristotle's system) are (P.i.15); again in terms of the distinction between the indubitable phenomenon and dubitable judgments about the relationship between the phenomenon and the underlying object (P.i.19), when he says that the Skeptic's doubt "does not concern the appearance itself but the account given of that appearance," thereby implying the Skeptic's repudiation of the doctrine of universal dubitability; again in terms of the distinction between facts (*pragmata*) experienced and recognized by all, including all philosophers and all mankind (P.i.210–11), and dogmas; again in terms of the distinction between facts "apparent to all men equally . . . acknowledged and uncontroverted" (P.ii.8) and the dogmas of philosophers interminably disputed. The Ten Tropes of Aenesidemus are, in Sextus' presentation, arguments designed to induce suspense-of-judgment with respect to the "nature of objects" (*tēs phuseos ton pragmaton*), but the evidential basis of each of the arguments— a set of observable facts about animal variety, human differences, sensory differences, sensory circumstances, and so on—is taken to be apparent to all men equally and exempted from suspense-of-judgment (P.i.36–163). The same is the case with respect to the Five Tropes of Agrippa (P.i.164–77) and the Two Tropes "handed down by the older Skeptics" (P.i.178–79): the suspense-of-judgment they are designed to induce is not taken to be applicable to their evidential bases. Again, when discussing the differences and similarities between the Skeptic Way (*agogē*) and the Heraclitean *philosophias*—a discussion which could not even begin if *epochē* were universally applicable, to say nothing of skepticism in Hamlyn's sense—Sextus notes that the Heracliteans start from the same general (or common, or universal) preconceptions of mankind, "just as we also do," and that "their starting-points are impressions experienced not by us only but by all the other philosophers and by ordinary man," all of us making use of "the same common material" (P.i.211).

It is not only to such evident and indubitable empirical facts, not matters of philosophical controversy, that Sextus appeals throughout his fourteen books; it is also to logical facts—logical impossibilities, certainties, validities, invalidities, and the underlying general principles: to the law of the excluded middle (P.ii.86, 88, 90; iii.33, 40–41, 132, 138–39); to the law of contradiction (P.ii.143; L.ii.52–53); to the fallacy of circular reasoning (L.ii.22); to the principle of self-refutation (L.i.389); to the impossibility of an infinite series (P.ii.85); and in a single short passage to the principle of self-refutation, the law of the excluded middle, and the technique of *reductio ad absurdum* (L.ii.55–57). There is much more of the same kind—all overlooked by those who read Sextus as a general skeptic.[11]

The knowledge- and/or truth-claims made at every point in Sextus's corpus— for example, at the very outset of *Outlines,* where his numerous assertions (affirmations) are sometimes implicitly and sometimes explicitly also knowledge-and/or truth-claims (or are we to suppose that he does not think he knows of the existence of all the philosophers he describes and the character of all the philosophies he describes, including himself and Skepticism itself?)—are extended also to the Skeptic End (*telos*). About it—"that for which all actions or reasonings are undertaken, while it exists for the sake of none, the ultimate object of appetency" (P.i.25)—he writes, "We assert (*phamen*) still that the Skeptic's end is quietude (*ataraxian*) in respect of matters of opinion (*doxan*) and moderate feeling (*metriopatheian*) in respect of things unavoidable (*katenagkasmenois*)" (P.i.25–26), thus contradicting those interpretations which have the Skeptic refusing to say yes or no about anything (see section 2.1.2), or refusing to say anything about anything, or refusing to make affirmations or denials about anything, or holding that the Skeptic's End (according to Sextus) is just *ataraxia* (and then criticizing the doctrine on the basis of that misinterpretation).[12] There are categorical affirmations, and by implication truth-claims, about the nature and existence of the Skeptic End (P.i.25–26), the conditions under which it is attainable (P.i.26–29), unattainable (P.i.27), both (E.141–67), and—scattered throughout the work *Against the Ethicists*—a comparative and critical discussion of the ethical doctrines of the ethical philosophers and that of the Skeptics (E.i.257) involving affirmative judgments, positive and negative, throughout.

2.1.2.2 *The counterevidence.* The evidence or seeming evidence that one or another of our eleven theses about Sextus (section 2.1.2) is false falls into one or another of three groups: first, some of Sextus' own formulations of the Skeptic philosophy; second, the famous "Skeptic expressions or formulas"; and third, his categorical statement that there is no truth.[13]

To take up the first of these, Sextus' own formulations of the Skeptic philosophy: Sextus defines Skepticism as "an ability (or power) that opposes appearances to judgments in any way whatsoever, with the result that owing to the equipollence of the objects and reasons thus opposed, we are brought first to suspense-of-judgment and then to quietude" (P.i.8), that suspense-of-judgment then being explained as a state of mental rest "owing to which we neither deny or affirm anything" (P.i.10). It is evident, by inspection, that this definition (already an affirmation: an affirmation that this is what Skepticism is) is not a formulation of general skepticism: it does not assert that knowledge is impossible, and so on. In combination with the explanation of suspense-of-judgment, it has, however, been taken to be a formulation of both universal suspension of assertion and of belief.[14] The definition and the added explanation are taken at face value: the Skeptic is not to affirm or deny anything whatsoever, and he is not to make "judgments in any way whatsoever." But I have already adduced numerous general considerations to show that for Sextus the scope of his inquiry in general is limited, not unlimited; and it follows, if consistency is to be preserved, that the scope of his formulations has similarly to be limited, not unlimited. The judgments to which appearances are to be opposed are philosophical (or scientific or technical) judgments; the things or statements not to be affirmed or denied are philosophical (or . . .) things or statements. Suspension of belief and of assertion is not to be universal.

There are additional, more specific considerations in support of this interpretation. In the course of his explanations of Skepticism, Sextus writes, "The main basic principle of Skepticism is that of opposing to every proposition an equal proposition" (P.i.12), thus seeming once again to undermine *every* proposition and thus, given the context, to be advocating (but how, except by assertion?) universal suspense-of-judgment. But repeatedly he says—in passages which have been overlooked or ignored by many prominent students of Greek Skepticism— that formulations advanced by him which on the face of it are universal in scope are "elliptical" (P.i.188), that is, defective or incomplete, requiring to be filled out or qualified before they say more exactly what is intended. So when Sextus discusses a Skeptic formula similar in essential respects to the one quoted above ("To every proposition an equal proposition is opposed"), "To every argument an equal argument is opposed" (P.i.202), he explains in effect that it is *not* to be taken at face value: "We mean," he says, " 'to every argument' that has been investigated by us, and the word 'argument' we use not in its simplest sense, but of that which establishes a point dogmatically (that is to say with reference to what is non-evident)"; and he adds: "So whenever I say 'To every argument an equal argument is opposed,' what I am virtually saying is 'To every argument investigated by me which establishes a point dogmatically, it seems to me there is opposed another argument establishing a point dogmatically, which is equal to the first in respect of credibility and incredibility'; so that the utterance of the phrase is not a piece of dogmatism, but the announcement of a human state of mind which is apparent to the person experiencing it" (P.i.203). So whenever he says, "To every proposition an equal proposition is opposed," he is not proposing a self-contradictory assertion that *no* assertion (denial or affirmation) is to be made, nor is he proposing the self-contradictory judgment that *all* judgment is to be suspended; he is saying that suspension of all assertion (affirmation or denial), of all judgment, and so of all knowledge-claims and truth-claims with respect to philosophical (or scientific or technical) matters (that is to say, claims about the nonevident) is warranted for reasons adduced, for example, in the Ten Tropes of Aenesidemus and in the Five Tropes of Agrippa. He is not advocating general skepticism in Hamlyn's or Annas and Barnes's sense; he is not advocating universal dubitability; he is not even advocating the universal suspense-of-judgment or of assertion.

The second of the groups of counterevidence, the Skeptic expressions or shorthand formulas, have also been taken by many to be formulations of general skepticism:[15] (1) "No more" (*ouden mallon* [P.i.188]); (2) "Non-assertion" (*aphasia* [P.i.192]); (3) "I suspend judgment" (*epecho* [P.i.196]); (4) "I determine nothing" (*ouden orizo* [P.i.197]); (5) "All things are undetermined" (or "undeter-minable" [?]; *panta estin aorista*[P.i.198]); (6) "All things are inapprehensible" (or "unapprehended" [?]; *panta estin akatalēpta* [P.i.200]);[16] (7) "I am non-apprehending" and "I apprehend not" (*akatalēpto* and *ou katalamban* [P.i.201]); and (8) "To every argument an equal argument is opposed" (*panti logo logos isos antikētai* [P.i.202]).

Some of these shorthand formulas have been interpreted to be doubly or triply unrestricted in scope: all skeptics make no assertions about anything; I suspend all judgment about anything whatever; I determine nothing whatever with respect to any property whatever about anything whatever. Some have been interpreted (although rarely if ever so explicitly) to mean that I (for any I, presumably) apprehend nothing (for any *x*, with respect to any *F*,) and that all things, being inapprehensible, are unknowable. But none of these interpretations takes any account of the considerations, some quite general and others more specific, which I have presented so far. They fail to take account of further considerations Sextus introduces concerning these shorthand formulas. Right at the outset of his reference to those formulas (P.i.14), he says that they concern things nonevident, that is to say, the nonevident objects of scientific inquiry (P.i.13). They are *not* about everything: nonassertion, suspense-of-judgment, nondetermination (or indeterminability), inapprehension (or inapprehensibility), and so on are about and only about the nonevident objects of scientific inquiry.

When in chapters 18 through 28 of *Outlines* (P.i.187–209) Sextus presents an extended account of the shorthand formulas, he immediately explains that formula 1 is elliptical and that the Skeptic is "implicitly saying 'Not this more than that, up than down' " (P.i.188); that formula 2 is elliptical, implicitly meaning that "what we neither affirm nor deny is some one of the dogmatic statements made about what is non-evident" (P.i.193); and so for formulas 3 (P.i.196), 4 (P.i.197), 5 (P.i.198–99), and 6 (P.i.200)—formula 6 being especially interesting and significant because it is the formula which has most given rise to the interpretations of Greek Skepticism as a form of general skepticism. But formula 6, in the reformulation of Sextus, comes out as anything but a form of general skepticism: "All the non-evident matters of dogmatic inquiry which I have investigated appear to me inapprehensible" (P.i.200). His reformulation of formula 7 is also illuminating: "Both the expressions . . . are indicative of a personal state of mind in which the Skeptic, for the time being, avoids affirming or denying any non-evident matter of inquiry" (P.i.201). Note the phrase "for the time being" (an expression I myself used above, section 2.1.2): even the limited nonassertion doctrine is not temporally unconditional. I see no reason to suppose that any of the Skeptic formulas is not to be reformulated in the same temporally conditional terms; for he says as much in his further explanations of formula 6: "I conceive that *up until now* I myself have apprehended nothing" (P.i.200). All the characteristic doctrines of the Greek Skeptics, as limited in scope as I have found them to be, are, even so, "for the time being" only: a far cry from the general skepticism of Hamlyn and all the others, including Hegel and Hume.

The third of the groups of counterevidence concerns Sextus' statement that there is no truth. "Sextus," C. L. Stough writes, "declares unequivocally that nothing is true" (*ouden estin alēthes* [P.ii.85; L.ii.17–18]), and she concludes that the tradition of unqualified skepticism begun by Pyrrho "received its fullest expression in the philosophy of Sextus Empiricus."[17] All the considerations we have so far adduced—none of which she takes account of in her consideration of the "nothing is true" formula—contradict her conclusion. But there is more to be said about this particular formula. Unequivocal it may be; but, like all the other shorthand formulas I have so far considered, unelliptical and therefore unconditional it is not. Although the formula is not listed and discussed in chapters 18 through 28 of *Outlines,* and so is not reformulated there as all the others are, it *is* mentioned when he first mentions those formulas and describes them as "the Skeptic formulas concerning things non-evident" (P.i.14), adding that "the Skeptic does not assert these formulas in any unconditional sense." It, like all the others, is an elliptical formulation; and about *all* of them he says that "we do not employ them universally about all things, but about those which are non-evident and are objects of dogmatic inquiry" (P.i. 207–8), an explanation exactly like that which he provides for the use of the term "all" in the shorthand formulas (P.i.198, 200).

2.1.3 *Pyrrho.* In the twentieth century, at least seven specialists in Greek Skepticism view Pyrrho as a general skeptic: R. G. Bury, D. W. Hamlyn, C. L. Stough, A. A. Long, D. N. Sedley, J. Barnes, and J. Annas.[18] Some among this group hold also that he rejected all belief, all assertion, and even all speech. As Pyrrho wrote nothing, there are no works of his which might be consulted in order to determine now whether he is or is not a general skeptic. At best in the form of paraphrase, all the surviving evidence about Pyrrho's views is at best secondhand and worse. One supposed earwitness was Timon of Phlius, and he supposedly gives an account of what has widely been interpreted to be Pyrrho's general skepticism in a report consisting of just six sentences. This "Pyrrho-text" is supposed to be part of a work of Timon's; but that work itself has not survived and so cannot now be consulted. The Pyrrho-text is nevertheless supposed to have been preserved in a work written—five centuries later!—by Aristocles in the second century A.D.: but that work too has not survived, and so it too cannot now be consulted. It is only in a still-surviving work, *Praeparatio Evangelica,* written—six centuries later—in the third century A.D. by the Christian Bishop Eusebius that the Pyrrho-text is preserved and that in the twentieth century must be consulted in order to try to determine what it was that Pyrrho said and thought: at a remove, thus, of six centuries and three persons, the first of whom, claiming to have heard the utterance of these views by Pyrrho, claims also only to have recorded them in paraphrase on the basis of his recollection of those utterances.[19]

None of this would matter very much if it were not the case that so very much hangs on it: the widespread interpretation in the twentieth century of epistemology as engendered by and even definable in terms of general skepticism. If we remember the lamentations of the likes of Russell and Quine—masters of English, all of whose numerous works are available for prolonged study—over the numerous misinterpretations and even misstatements of their published views, and if we remember also the endless conflicting interpretations of the works and utterances of Wittgenstein despite his accessibility to many of his interpreters, we can better appreciate the quicksand of the Pyrrho-text and of the precariousness not only of all interpretations of it but even of the translations of it, and especially of all those who claim subsequently to find a statement of general skepticism in it.[20]

Putting aside the questions of the authenticity and accuracy of the Pyrrho-text, I address the question of the philosophical content and significance of the text. To that end I reproduce the Greek text, and part of its context, and six translations of it, the first of which is a translation of the whole of the text and is also the most recent.

2.1.3.1 The entire Greek text, with its sentences numbered and the essential sentences underscored, reads as follows:

(1) ἀναγκαίως δ' ἔχει πρὸ παντὸς διασκέψασθαι περὶ τῆς ἡμῶν αὐτῶν γνώσεως· εἰ γὰρ αὖ μηδὲν πεφύκαμεν γνωρίζειν, οὐδὲν ἔτι δεῖ περὶ τῶν ἄλλων σκοπεῖν ἐγένοντο μὲν οὖν καὶ τῶν πάλαι τινὲς οἱ ἀφέντες τήνδε τὴν φωνήν, οἷς ἀντείρηκεν Ἀριστοτέλης. (2) ἴσχυσε μὲν τοιαῦτα λέγων καὶ Πύρρων ὁ Ἠλεῖος· ἀλλ' αὐτὸς μὲν οὐδὲν ἐν γραφῇ καταλέλοιπεν, ὁ δέ γε μαθητὴς αὐτοῦ Τίμων φησὶ δεῖν τὸν μέλλοντα εὐδαιμονήσειν εἰς τρία ταῦτα βλέπειν· πρῶτον μέν, <u>ὁποῖα πέφυκε τὰ πράγματα</u>· δεύτερον δέ, τίνα χρὴ τρόπον ἡμᾶς πρὸς αὐτὰ διακεῖσθαι· τελευταῖον δέ, τί περιέσται τοῖς οὕτως ἔχουσι. (3) <u>τὰ μὲν οὖν πράγματά φησιν αὐτὸν ἀποφαίνειν ἐπ' ἴσης ἀδιάφορα καὶ ἀστάθμητα καὶ ἀνεπίκριτα·</u> (4) <u>διὰ τοῦτο μήτε τὰς αἰσθήσεις ἡμῶν μήτε τὰς δόξας ἀληθεύειν ἢ ψεύδεσθαι.</u> διὰ τοῦτο οὖν μηδὲ πιστεύειν αὐταῖς δεῖν, ἀλλ' ἀδοξάστους καὶ ἀκλινεῖς καὶ ἀκραδάντους εἶναι, <u>περὶ ἑνὸς ἑκάστου λέγοντας ὅτι οὐ μᾶλλον ἔστιν ἢ οὐκ ἔστιν ἢ καὶ ἔστι καὶ οὐκ ἔστιν ἢ οὔτε ἔστιν οὔτε οὐκ ἔστιν.</u> (5) τοῖς μέντοι γε διακειμένοις οὕτω περιέσεσθαι Τίμων φησὶ πρῶτον μὲν ἀφασίαν, ἔπειτα δ' ἀταραξίαν, Αἰνησίδημος δ' ἡδονήν. (6) τὰ μὲν οὖν κεφάλαια τῶν λεγομένων ἐστὶ ταῦτα.[21]

2.1.3.2 The six translations, keyed to the sentences in the Greek, are as follows:

1. "[(1) It is supremely necessary to investigate our own capacity for knowledge. For if we are so constituted that we know nothing there is no need to continue enquiry into other things. Among the ancients too there have

been people who made this pronouncement, and Aristotle has argued against them. (2) Pyrrho of Elis was also a powerful spokesman of such a position. He himself has left nothing in writing, but his pupil Timon says that whoever wants to be happy must consider these three questions: first, how are things by nature? Secondly, what attitude should we adopt towards them? Thirdly, what will be the outcome for those who adopt this attitude? (3) According to Timon, Pyrrho declared that things are equally indifferent, unmeasurable and inarbitrable. (4) For this reason neither our sensations nor our opinions tell us truths or falsehoods. Therefore for this reason we should not put our trust in them one bit, saying concerning each individual thing that it no more is than is not, or it both is and is not, or it neither is nor is not. (5) The outcome for those who actually adopt this attitude, says Timon, will be first speechlessness, and then freedom from disturbance; [and Aenesidemus says pleasure. (6) These are the main points of what they say.][22]

2. (2) What is the nature of things? . . . (3) Things are in an equal degree indifferent and unstable and incapable of being tested. (4) For this reason neither our senses nor our opinions are true or false.[23]

3. (2) What is the nature of things? . . . (3) . . . things are by nature equally indeterminable, admitting of neither measurement nor discrimination. (4) For this reason, our sense experiences and beliefs are neither true nor false.[24]

4. (2) What things are really like . . . . (3) . . . things are equally indistinguishable, unmeasurable, and indeterminable. (4) For this reason neither our acts of perception nor our judgments are true or false.[25]

5. (2) . . . What are things like by nature? (3) [The world is in its own nature] undifferentiated, unmeasurable and unjudgeable.[26]

6. (2) . . . what objects are like by nature. . . . (3) . . . objects are equally indifferent and unfathomable and undeterminable. . . . (4) . . . neither our senses nor our judgments are true or false.[27]

2.1.3.3 When these six translations are presented side by side for inspection, it is evident—although it might otherwise not be—that translation is already interpretation: that a measure of interpretation, sometimes decisive, is embodied in the very translations themselves. It is not as though we were presented with two reasonably distinct processes consisting first of neutral or interpretation-free translation from one language to another and second of interpretation in terms of the second language. In the case of every crucial term, the two processes have been fused. On top of that a second layer of interpretation has been superimposed over the whole.

I shall do three things with respect to these six translations: first, point out more or less radical conflicts among the senses with which they endow the Greek text; second, indicate the unintelligibility of some of the translations; and third, argue that all are in one crucial respect or another unwarranted and therefore that the interpretations based on them—that Pyrrho denied the possibility of knowledge and rejected all belief, assertion, and even speech—are unwarranted. The evidence warranting the judgment that Pyrrho is a general skeptic (and so forth) is woefully insufficient, and the evidence that he is not is overwhelming. On the basis of my examination of Sextus Empiricus and of Pyrrho I propose principles of interpretation with which to deal with the remaining supposed general skeptics.

First, the conflicting senses suggested by the translations: Only in translations 2 and 3 is the first of the three questions (which according to Timon must be considered by the person who seeks happiness) rendered in the same way: "What is the nature of things?" In translation 1 it comes out as "How are things by nature?"; in translation 4 as "What are things really like?"; and in translations 5 and 6 in essentially the same way, "What are things (or objects) like by nature?" What we find, then, is the central and crucial question in the Greek text rendered in three essentially different ways. The first of these three ways is the only natural rendering of the Greek. There is no word in the Greek for the "how" of translation 1, the "by nature" of the same translation, the "really like" of translation 4, or the "like" (and again the "by nature") of translations 5 and 6. All these translations, besides being gratuitous interpolations of what is not to be found in the Greek, obliterate the force of the original question, which is about the nature of things and is the central question of all pre-Socratic philosophy that almost all if not all of the pre-Socratics undertook more or less explicitly to answer.[28] To ask "*How* are things by nature?"—if it makes any sense at all—is not to ask "What is *the nature* of things?" That is equally true of "What are things really like?" in which the reference to the nature of things is completely omitted, and of "What are things like by nature?" and "What are objects like by nature?" Indeed, the last two renderings make no sense at all. And the link with the great question of pre-Socratic philosophy is obscured when it is not wholly lost.

Pyrrho's fundamental answer to the first of the three questions is given in sentence 3 of the Greek text. The essential part of it has a subject and a predicate. According to all the translations except number 5, the subject is "things" or "objects"; in translation 5 it is "the world"—a difference of immense significance in metaphysics. Be that as it may, however, the original question is not about things *or* the world; it is about *the nature* of things—again a difference of immense significance in metaphysics.

The differences among the translations on the side of the predicate of sentence 3 are quite as radical. The predicate of the sentence contains three crucial verbal adjectives of the kind known as *alpha-privatives: adiaphora, astathmēta,* and *anepikrita.* In translations 1, 2, and 6 *adiaphora* is rendered as "indifferent," in translation 3 as "indeterminable," in translation 4 as "indistinguishable," and in translation 5 as "undifferentiated." Sedley's translation, number 5, is so far a metaphysical proposition;[29] Stough's, number 3, is so far an epistemological proposition; and Long's, number 4, is so far either indeterminately metaphysical—if "indistinguishable" is to be construed (though Long does not say how it is to be construed) as saying something about a general absence of distinguishable features in reality itself—or epistemological, if "indistinguishable" is to be construed as saying something about a general human incapacity for making cognitive distinctions.

As for *astathmēta,* it is rendered as "unmeasurable" in translations 1, 3, 4, and 5, but as "unstable" in translation 2 and as "unfathomable" in translation 6. But none of these renderings implies or is implied by any of the others; and clearly they attribute radically different properties to things, yielding radically different doctrines on the basis of a single Greek sentence (and only part of it, at that).

Anepikrita is not spared: it comes out as "inarbitrable" in translation 1, "incapable of being tested" in 2, "indiscriminable" in 3, and "indeterminable" in the remaining three translations: once again, four different philosophical doctrines on the basis of (part of) a single Greek sentence. Strangely, except for Burnet, whose translation precedes the earliest of all the others by decades, none of these translators makes any reference to any of the earlier translations, as if there were not a serious problem of translation.

In respect to the second point, I would argue that most of the translations are in some part unintelligible. The first translation's "*How* are things by nature?"— to say nothing of the fact that *hopoia* means, not "how," but "what" or "of what kind," as it is in translations 2 and 3, for example—is an unintelligible question. According to the *Oxford English Dictionary,* to ask "How is (or are) X (or Xs)?" is to ask in what way or manner is X or by what means is X. But the question so construed makes even less sense, if possible, when "by nature" is affixed to it: "In what way are things *by nature?*" "In what manner are things *by nature?*" "By what means are things *by nature?*" These are unintelligible concatenations of words. Even the sense of "how" in the context of a question about the general state of affairs, say, in the Middle East, where an intelligible answer would be "frightful," an intelligible question becomes unintelligible as soon as "by nature" is affixed to it. It makes no sense—although it is not meaningless—to say that the state of affairs in the world or in some part of the world is *by nature* frightful. And if the question as formulated in translation 1 could be made sense of, the fundamental answer given is irrelevant to the question asked: we are not told how things are (whether by nature or otherwise) when we are told that they are equally indifferent, unmeasurable, and inarbitrable. Either, therefore, the "answer" given to the question posed makes no sense, or the question posed makes no sense given the answer. The question arises, therefore, whether the unintelligibility of the question as formulated is an accurate reflection of the Greek original. I see no reason to believe that it is.

If translation 1's formulation of the fundamental question makes no sense, its formulation of the fundamental answer makes none either. It makes no sense to say that *things* are inarbitrable (or arbitrable): the category of arbitrability is inapplicable to things; it is applicable only to human conflict, disputes, disagreements, and the like (as in the Latin original of the word). Burnet's formulation of the fundamental answer, in translation 2, is equally unintelligible. It makes no sense to say that things are incapable of being tested: the category of testability is inapplicable to things, being applicable only to conjectured characterizations of things. Such considerations are equally applicable to the translations by Stough, Long, Sedley, and Annas and Barnes. With all these formulations, our earlier question arises again: Is the unintelligibility of these formulations of the fundamental answer an accurate reflection of the Greek original, or is it something superimposed on the latter by way of a translation cut to the cloth of general skepticism?

The third point concerns the warrant for the translations. Of all the translators, only Stough advances a justification of her translation of the fundamental answer (sentence 3 translation 3) to the fundamental question (sentence 2). The rest advance their translations as if there were nothing controversial or questionable about them, and as if there were nothing controversial or questionable about the interpretations based on those translations (the translations themselves already embodying interpretations). (The most recent interpretation—in the massive two-volume study by A. A. Long and D. N. Sedley—begins with early Pyrrhonism, that is to say with Pyrrho, about whom the authors reproduce accounts from a number of ancient sources, and then devote three large pages of fine print to philosophical commentary and interpretation—with not a word about their translations. Annas and Barnes too find nothing in their translation of the Pyrrho-text which merits comment, discussion, or justification.)

Stough begins her extended discussion of her translation (*Greek Skepticism,* 17–34) with her translation of *adiaphora,* "indeterminable." Acknowledging that the term's sentential context is capable of more than one interpretation, she concludes (by questionable reasoning) that the meaning of sentence 3 is that "the nature of things cannot be known" (18), "thus at the very outset a statement of Pyrrho's skepticism," which she earlier (4) interprets as general skepticism. *Adiaphora* she treats as the fundamental term in sentence 3; *astathmēta* and *anepikrita* she views as explanatory of *adiaphora* (18 n. 5). Recognizing that it was used by the early Stoics in an ethical context to apply to entities or acts that are neither good nor bad but "indifferent," she then claims that in sentence 3 the term has the extended sense (though she does not put it so) of *aphasia,* "non-assertion," the refusal to affirm (accept) or deny (reject) anything (the doctrine we have already seen in Sextus, and seen misinterpreted), remaining neutral "for the reasons supplied by *astathmēta* and *anepikrita*."

But what justification is there for thinking that in sentence 3 the term *adiaphora* has the extended sense which she translates as "indeterminable" and then interprets as "unknowable"? I argue above that it makes no sense to say of things, one by one or collectively, that they are indeterminable; I contend here that there is nothing in sentence 3 or in the whole Pyrrho-text or in any other source of information about Pyrrho (e.g., the extended account supplied by Diogenes Laertius) that warrants her translation and interpretation of *adiaphora*.

To begin at the beginning, *adiaphora* (like *astathmēta* and *anepikrita*) is a verbal adjective of the kind classified in classical Greek grammars as an alpha-privative. It is a derivative of the verb *diaphēro* (with the negating alpha prefixed), whose basic sense is *to differ* or *to be different from* (Liddell and Scott, *Greek-English Lexicon*). Thus, *adiaphora*'s basic meaning is "not different" in contexts such as *x is not different from y* (in this or that respect). The term does indeed have an extended sense: for example, in the early Stoics whose ethical doctrine distinguished three classes of acts—the ethically good, bad, and indifferent or neutral (neither good nor bad). Sextus himself notes that the term is used in three senses: in the first, of that which is an object of neither inclination nor disinclination: in the second, of that which, though it is an object of inclination or disinclination, is not particularly such an object; and in the third, of that which contributes neither to happiness nor unhappiness (P.iii.177). Nowhere, however, does he recognize the sense given to it by Stough and then interpreted as "unknowable." For "indeterminable" there are other terms in Greek.

In the *Greek-English Lexicon* (unabridged; the abridged twenty-sixth edition supplies only two senses), Liddell and Scott list five different meanings in English for *adiaphora:* "Not different," "indifferent," "undiscriminating," "indistinguishable," and "having no logical differentia." Since "indeterminable" is not among them, the question is where Stough got it and how. It will not do to say that Long's "indistinguishable" (in translation 4, sentence 3) and Sedley's "undifferentiated" (in translation 5, sentence 3) are close enough. Stough's "indeterminable" has a different meaning and conveys a different doctrine, and such terms have to be used with great care in a philosophical context. What justifies going from "indistinguishable," which is supplied by Liddell and Scott, to "indeterminable," which is not? And why suppose that Pyrrho himself meant "unknowable" or "indeterminable" or "indistinguishable" instead of the simpler and more natural "indifferent" used in translations 1, 2 and 6? He was famous, indeed notorious, in his day for his detachment from all matters and so for the degree to which he had attained *ataraxia*, in some measure a consequence of the influence of Indian spiritual masters he is reported to have met in India when he accompanied Alexander the Great during the latter's military campaign into the Punjab.

The interpretive translations of the six translators seem as objectionable and questionable at many other points as I have made them out to be at the points already considered; but as I lack the space to deal with them all in detail, I must now deal with all the translations in more general terms. Questions arise about the Pyrrho-text and its translations which do not seem to have arisen—there being no evidence that they have—in the minds of any of the translators. If Pyrrho-Timon had meant to say in Greek what some of our translators have him saying in English—that things are indeterminable—why did he not say so in Greek? There are words—for example, *aoristos* ("unbounded, indefinite, indeterminate, indeterminable" in Liddell and Scott)—that in fact Sextus uses (see section 2.1.2, formula) to convey just this sense, which Pyrrho-Timon might have used to say, quite explicitly, that all things are indeterminable. Why take the strange course of using *adiaphora*, which does not obviously mean "indeterminable" and which, to the best of my knowledge, no other Greek philosopher uses in that sense?

There is a more fundamental question. Anyone who inspects the six translations without preconceptions can see that in none of them does Pyrrho-Timon say that knowledge is impossible, and so forth, or that truth is unattainable, and so forth. If Pyrrho-Timon had meant to say that the nature of things is unknowable (which, not so incidentally, does not entail saying that *things* are unknowable: I can know innumerable men without knowing the nature of man; innumerable material objects without knowing the nature of matter; innumerable works of art without knowing the nature of art; innumerable works of philosophy without knowing the nature of philosophy), why did he not say so in so many words? The text contains no knowledge-terms at all. Why, therefore, use *adiaphora* (or *astathmēta*, or *anepikrita*) when those terms cannot by any stretch of the imagination be used to convey a knowledge-proposition, and above all when the Greek language of his time and for centuries earlier had the resources to convey just such propositions: *gnosis, agnoston, ismen, gignoskein,* and *eidenai,* among others? Using these terms and/or others, he could have said that knowledge is impossible, and so forth, or that truth is unattainable, and so forth. Such epistemic terms were in wide use by Greek philosophers both in his time and long before his time by Aristotle, Plato, the early Stoics, Democritus, Xenophanes, and Metrodorus. Some of them—for example, Metrodorus of Chios—had even used one or the other of these terms to convey what has been interpreted by many scholars and philosophers as a form of general skepticism: "None of us knows anything, not even the very fact whether we know or do not know; nor do we know what it is not to know or to know, nor in general whether anything is or is not" (cf. L.i.88 for the Greek text of the first half of the quotation; and note the echoes in sentence 4 of the Greek of Pyrrho-Timon). Gorgias had used other terms to convey what has been interpreted by many scholars and philosophers as another form of general skepticism: "first, nothing exists; second, even if anything exists it is inapprehensible by man; and third, even if anything is apprehensible, it is certainly inexpressible and incommunicable to one's neighbor" (L.i.65–6), which Sextus then reformulates—I reproduce only the relevant second clause—as "even if anything exists it is unknowable (*agnoston*) and inconceivable (*anepinoēton*) by man" (L.i.77: one of the rare texts, cited in its original form—L.i.65—by Hamlyn in *The Theory of Knowledge* [8 n. 1], where he evidently takes it at face value). Metrodorus is a fourth-century figure, and Gorgias takes us back into the fifth. According to all the accounts available to us, all this was known to Pyrrho—both the epistemic terms and the Greek philosophers who used these and other epistemic terms to formulate epistemological doctrine, skeptical or not. Timon, a personal acquaintance, attributes knowledge of Sophists to Pyrrho in his *Pytho* and *Silli* (cf. *Diogenes Laertius*, Loeb Classical Library [2:479] and the account of Pyrrho's life [2: chap. 11]). Yet Pyrrho makes no use of any of it in the text widely interpreted (after what in my judgment is unwarranted translation) as a declaration of general skepticism. That is not credible.

The Pyrrho-text does indeed contain some epistemic and semantic terms: *aisthēsis, doxas, aleithuein,* and *pseudesthae*. But even with the help of these the text does not say in so many words that knowledge is impossible, that truth is unattainable, that nothing is true (as in fact Sextus does), or that everything is false, and so on, ringing all the changes we will. What it says at most is that two things—two classes of things: *aisthēsis* and *doxas*—are neither true nor false; but no matter how anyone translates these two terms ("sense experience" and "belief" respectively, by Stough; "senses" and "opinions" by Burnet; "sensations" and "opinions" by Long and Sedley; or "senses" and "judgments" by Annas and Barnes), the interpretation of the whole text as a statement of general skepticism would be justified only if in addition we knew that according to Pyrrho-Timon *aisthēsis* were the sole source or means of knowledge and *doxas* the sole means of expressing it. But that is just what—to go by the given text or indeed by any additional information or speculation provided by Diogenes Laertius, Aristocles, Cicero, Seneca, and above all by Sextus Empiricus—we cannot know: the text advances no generalization to the effect that knowledge is obtainable, if obtainable at all, solely by means of *aisthēsis,* and that it is expressible, if expressible at all, solely in terms of *doxas*.

That the inference does make, or imply, such a generalization is speculation unwarranted by any evidence available in the text or anywhere else. For example, everyone who reads the Pyrrho-text in terms of general skepticism and cites a certain text from Timon cites it as evidence of Pyrrho's general skepticism: "Aged Pyrrho, how and whence did you find escape from slavery to the opinions and empty thought of the sophists and break the bonds of all deceit and persuasion? You were not concerned to inquire what winds blow over Greece, and the origin and destination of each thing."[30] But to interpret this Timon-text as a statement of general skepticism is again unwarranted: escape from slavery to the opinions of the Sophists and unconcern about such physical and metaphysical questions as those about the winds blowing over Greece and about the origins and destination of each thing (these being questions central in the inquiries of the pre-Socratics, first and foremost among the Milesians) is evidence not of general skepticism—where are the denials of the possibility of knowledge?—but of a certain detachment from sophistical views and physical-metaphysical inquiries of just the "dogmatic" kind which Sextus is concerned to repudicate as futile and unresolved if not unresolvable.

It is likewise unwarranted to claim that the Pyrrho-text entails that further inquiry about the world need not even commence once the truth about the world—"that it is in its own nature undifferentiated, unmeasurable, and unjudgeable"[31]—has been announced: this interpretation contradicts everything else that is reported about Pyrrho: for example, that he traveled to India with Alexander the Great for the express purpose of inquiring about the world of Indian culture; that he made fundamental changes in his mode of life as a consequence of what he heard—unveridically?—an Indian saying to his companion Anaxarchus;[32] and that by Diogenes' account Pyrrho does all the things he is supposed to have eschewed as a general skeptic—*makes* judgments, *makes* assertions, *makes* discriminations, distinctions, and determinations—as indeed it is quite impossible to avoid doing.

This interpretation contradicts even the very Pyrrho-text itself, which does what, according to a number of translations, the text is supposed to be saying cannot be done: discriminates between *aisthēsis* and *doxas,* between *alēthuein* and *pseudesthai,* between *adiaphora* and *astathmēta* and *anepikrita,* between *aphasia* and *phasis,* and between *ataraxia* and *taraxis.* If the world were, as Pyrrho-Timon is supposed to be saying and believing that it is, an undifferentiated and featureless blob, on what possible basis could he be making the discriminations and distinctions which he everywhere unfailingly makes? If Pyrrho had rejected *all* belief and even assertion (Annas and Barnes), what was he doing in—and how are we to construe—the Pyrrho-text itself? And if he was supposed to have advised and adopted speechlessness (Long and Sedley, Hamlyn, Burnet), how could he have advised it without speech, and how, after having advised and adopted it, could he have continued chattering so cheerfully to the end of his ninety years? None of this makes any sense on the basis of general skepticism (except on the further supposition that Pyrrho was so unobservant that he failed in ninety years to detect his gross inconsistencies); but it makes the best of sense on our interpretation of Sextus and of his interpretation of Pyrrho. But all these inconsistencies and discrepancies are created by the translations; they are not to be found in the Greek text itself.

There is a still more fundamental general question, relevant to all classical Greek texts whether philosophical or not (e.g., poetic, dramatic, or narrative), to which I must now address myself. I have hitherto allowed Hamlyn's fourth version of general skepticism—that we never know anything (cf. Metrodorus' "None of us knows anything . . .")—to pass without comment; but it must now be said that the formulation is unacceptable as a version of general skepticism.[33] General skepticism in any philosophically significant sense must be formulated in modal terms—for example, in the version that knowledge is impossible or in the version that truth is unattainable. It is for that reason among others that the six translators have Pyrrho maintaining that things are indetermin*able*, unmeasur*able*, inarbitr*able*, untest*able*, indiscrimin*able*, unjudge*able*, unfathom*able*, and so on. If they had translated the Greek as undetermin*ed*, unmeasur*ed*, unarbitrat*ed*, untest*ed*, undiscriminat*ed*, unjudg*ed*, unfathom*ed*, and so on, the doctrinal outcome would not be general skepticism in any philosophically significant sense but mere ignorance—contingent, temporary, circumstantial, and superable: the situation of any ordinary or scientific investigator who for the time being has not determined, measured, arbitrated, tested, discriminated, judged, or fathomed whatever it is that he is investigating. Hence the modal terms and the modal formulations.

All these considerations are linked to a strange feature of classical Greek. It is a feature unmentioned by any of the six translator-interpreters or in any other literature known to me that deals with the culture (philosophical, poetic, dramatic, narrative, scientific, religious, etc.) of ancient Greece,[34] and so neither these translators nor any other student of ancient Greek or Hellenistic philosophy takes account of it in his translations and interpretations (e.g., A. E. Taylor, W. K. C. Guthrie, F. M. Cornford, G. E. L. Owen, Kirk and Raven, and J. Barnes). In English, French, and Latin there are (although not invariably even in these languages) distinctive linguistic means of indicating the difference in meaning between verbs and their related or derived verbal adjectives: in English, *educate* and *educable, extricate* and *extricable, discover* and *discoverable, experience* and *experienceable, perceive* and *perceivable, know* and *knowable;* in French *inconnu* and *inconnaissable;* in Latin *indeterminatus* and *indeterminabilis*. In classical Greek that is not the case: one linguistic form serves for two or more distinct meanings, depending upon context—*abatos* for "untrodden," "not to be trodden," and "inaccessible"; *aneureton* for "not found out" (as a matter of fact), "not to be found out" (forbidden?), and "undiscoverable" (in principle beyond the reach of the discoverer-to-be); *adiaphora* for "not different" (as a matter of fact), "indifferent" (psychologically), "neutral" (ethically), and "indistinguishable" (in principle beyond the capacity of the perceiver-to-be to distinguish); *anepikrita* for "undecided" (as a matter of fact) and "undecidable" (in principle beyond the capacity of the decider-to-be); *agnoston* for "unknown" (as a matter of contingent fact) and "unknowable" (in principle beyond the reach of the knower-to-be).

This means that, unlike English, French, and Latin, classical Greek (not the Koine of the New Testament or the demotic of modern Greece) lacks distinctive linguistic forms to express the distinct meanings expressed by the pairs *undiscovered* and *undiscoverable, undetermined* and *indeterminable, unapprehended* and *inapprehensible, unconceived* and *inconceivable, uncommunicated* and *incommunicable, undecided* and *undecidable* (or *unresolved* and *unresolvable*), *untested* and *untestable, unknown* and *unknowable,* and so on for all the alpha-privatives, or at any rate for all those I have checked, which number in the scores. This is not to say that classical Greek is incapable of expressing such modal meanings— for example, that reality is unknowable or that truth is undiscoverable. On the contrary. But when it does so and does so unambiguously, it does so first by means of locutions (e.g., "the truth *can*not be apprehend*ed*" [P.i.2]) which can then be legitimately and acceptably equated with assertions formulated in terms of the related verbal adjectives, especially in their alpha-privative form (e.g., *akatalēpton,* "unapprehended" or "inapprehensible"), which otherwise are ambiguous or equivocal.

These facts about classical Greek are of the utmost importance in the assessment of the philosophical significance of the Pyrrho-text and indeed of all texts like it in the relevant respects (e.g., that of Metrodorus of Chios already quoted and that of Gorgias). Given a sentence like number 3 in the Pyrrho-text, how translate and then interpret it? The three crucial predicate-terms in it are alpha-privative verbal adjectives: *adiaphora, astathmēta,* and *anepikrita.* All three have been translated modally by almost all six translators. But the three words are equally translatable nonmodally: *undetermined* instead of *indeterminable,* and so on. How, then, decide which it is to be? On that decision hangs the interpretation of the sentence, and of all sentences like it, as a statement of general skepticism.

I have already indicated the answer: the decision can be made solely in terms of the context of the sentence—contexts like that (but not only like that) which I cite in the case of a text of Sextus. Although he uses alpha-privatives in sentences that, out of context, in isolation, are ambiguous and translatable in the very different ways already noted, he in fact uses them in contexts which make it clear—because the idea is expressed in terms of other locutions that are themselves unambiguous—that the alpha-privative is to be translated modally. But such a context is precisely what is lacking in the Pyrrho-text (hence my emphasis upon the extreme brevity of the text): there are no other sentences in the text that do not use alpha-privatives and that nevertheless convey the modal sentential meanings by means of modal terms which, according to all six translators (and all those other interpreters, like Hamlyn and Russell, who provide no translation), sentence number 3 conveys. I conclude, then, that there is no textual or other evidence justifying these modal translations, and therefore no justification for the subsequent interpretation of the whole text as a statement of general skepticism.

2.1.4 *Four principles of interpretation.* In section 2.1 I have so far examined the prime exhibits among the ancient skeptics in achronological order: the last of the Greek Skeptics first, and the first of them last. There are two very important reasons for such order. The first is that in the case of Sextus, uniquely, there is an enormous mass of primary data (four volumes' worth in the Loeb edition) on the solid basis of which to formulate a conception of the Skeptics' (and especially Sextus') philosophical outlook; there is nothing even remotely comparable in the case of all the remaining Greek Skeptics and the others. The second is that the very plethora of data in the case of Sextus and the dearth of data in the case of Pyrrho suggests principles of interpretation with the help of which we can more soundly interpret such texts, so ambiguous and difficult to interpret, as that of Pyrrho-Timon and, indeed, of all the remaining prime exhibits (and all such texts whether philosophical or not, for that matter).[35]

In the Pyrrho-text there are just six sentences, only four of which are directly relevant to my present concerns, just two of which are central, and only one of which is at the very center of the center. Consider now what the predicament of translators and interpreters of Sextus would have been if the textual data had been as minimal and meager as the Pyrrho-Timon data are. I divided the Sextus data into two classes: those that seem to support my eleven theses and those that seem to contradict them. Then I pointed out that Sextus advances numerous formulas— not just one, or two, or four, or six, but a great many more—some of which (but only some of which) have been cited by those who interpret him as a general skeptic. The extraordinary and startling fact is that it is possible, out of the mass of data available in the Sextus corpus, to select four sentences and to construct a "Sextus-text" which corresponds almost perfectly to the Pyrrho-text. Almost certainly, in the absence of all the other data I have adduced in support of my eleven theses, the conclusion would have been drawn by almost everyone—as it has with respect to Pyrrho—that Sextus is a general skeptic: and almost certainly that conclusion would have been erroneous, if all the counterconsiderations adduced in the course of our enquiry are what I say they are.

What is it, then, that makes it possible to avoid that conclusion (which I have resisted and questioned, in the first place, fundamentally because it is incredible)? In the broadest terms, two things: Sextus' own practice and his own explanations (section 2.1.2.1 and interspersed throughout section 2.1.2.2). On the explanatory side there are four things of crucial importance: definitions of key doctrines and key terms; explanations that do not amount to full definitions of key doctrines and key terms; a very large number of concrete examples and illustrations; and, overall, a comprehensive context consisting of thousands of assertions, judgments, and explanations systematically set forth, in the light of which interpretation is greatly facilitated.

The four principles of interpretation—to be quite explicit—are formulable, then, as follows: If an isolated philosophical text is to be adequately interpreted and even translated, then at least four conditions must be satisfied: first, the key doctrines and key terms must be identified and defined; second, in the absence of such definitions, explanations that approximate definitions for such key doctrines and key terms must be provided; third, whether definitions and explanations are or are not provided, concrete examples and illustrations of various important aspects of the doctrine must be provided, the more examples and illustrations of the more aspects the better; and fourth and finally, the isolated text must be embedded in the context of a comprehensive and systematic text. Without the satisfaction of these conditions, at the very least, the translation and subsequent interpretation (or just interpretation, if the interpreter and the interpreted are using the same language) of an isolated philosophical text is little better than educated guesswork. We can see such guesswork operating in scholarly and philosophical attempts to translate and then to interpret the Ionians, the Pythagoreans, the Eleatics, and the Sophists, some of whose surviving fragments form a total text far more extensive than that of the Pyrrho-text; and we can see it operating where philosophers such as Spinoza, Hegel, Whitehead, and Wittgenstein are concerned, whose published works form a total text incomparably greater in extent and hardly less obscure than the Pyrrho-text.

Not one of the four principles of interpretation—which I would be inclined to call obvious, except that they seem never to have been noticed or formulated before—is satisfied by that text. Whatever the key doctrines and terms are, none of them is defined, none of them is explained, none of them is illustrated by example, and no context—certainly no comprehensive and systematic context— is provided. What does Pyrrho-Timon mean when he asks, *hopoia pephuke ta pragmata?* The problem in this case is not one of translation: the correct translation is unquestionably, in my judgment, that of Burnet and Stough. The problem is what the translated question means. The text provides no explanation. What, when he/they say that things are equally *adiaphora?* The text provides no explanation. What, when it says that things are equally *astathmēta?* The text provides no explanation. What, when it says that things are equally *anepikrita?* The text provides no explanation. When, on the basis of the central assertion in the text (section 3), the text goes on to say (sentence 4) that neither *aisthēsis* nor *doxa* is true or false, how are we to understand these key terms and key denials? Neither *aisthēsis* nor *doxa* is defined or explained in the text itself, nor are they illustrated by means of examples in the text itself; and none of Pyrrho's contemporaries or near-contemporaries or interested later commentators—Timon, Diogenes Laertius, Cicero, Seneca, and others—supplies definitions, explanations, or illustrations.

What are we to take to be the scope or extension of these terms? Does every possible assertion we make—for example, the assertion by Pyrrho that he accompanied Alexander the Great on his military expedition of conquest to India, and all those by Pyrrho reported in the extended account by Diogenes Laertius, and for that matter all those recorded in the Pyrrho-Timon text itself—fall into the category of *doxa*? Does every possible mode of apprehension of which we seem to be capable (the apprehension of physical objects by sense, of logical relations by reason, of our own states of consciousness by intuition, and so on) fall into the category of *aisthēsis*, or is it the only or only possible mode of apprehension, according to Pyrrho-Timon? If the latter (as the six interpreters clearly think), then how are we to construe the statement that things are equally *adiaphora*, and so on, and the two following inferences that neither *aisthēsis* nor *doxa* has any truth value and that we should not trust either (a statement and inferences which the six interpreters do not undertake to explain)? Does the statement that things are equally *adiaphora*, and so on, itself have any truth value and cognitive value? Does the statement that neither *aisthēsis* nor *doxa* has any truth value itself have any truth and cognitive value? What about the statement that the outcome for those who adopt the recommended attitude will be *ataraxia*? How are we supposed to construe that? Is *it* supposed to be true? And if so, only true but not known or even believed to be true? We can only stumble blindly in a pitch-black swamp, sinking deeper with every step.

Given the context—or lack of it—these questions are bottomless, unanswerable in the absence of the satisfaction of the four principles of interpretation. But they arise only on the ground that Pyrrho is a general skeptic; they are otherwise groundless, and do not arise on our interpretation of Sextus and Sextus' interpretation in turn of Pyrrho.

2.1.5 *The remaining "general skeptics": a short-cut through them.* If I were to deal with the remaining prime exhibits among the supposed general skeptics in the ancient world as I have dealt with Sextus Empiricus and Pyrrho, the length of this study would become intolerable. Fortunately, there is a shortcut through all of them by way of the four principles of interpretation. It consists in the following claim: if the principles of interpretation elicited in my examination of Sextus and applied to Pyrrho are applied to any of the remaining supposed general skeptics, the conclusion is the same as it was for Sextus and Pyrrho—that the interpretation of them as general skeptics is mistaken, being unwarranted by the available evidence and ruled out by application of the four principles. In the case of Metrodorus of Chios, for example—whose single surviving sentence Barnes cites, quotes, takes at its face value, and unhesitatingly interprets as a statement of general skepticism[36]—I unhesitatingly repudiate the interpretation in accordance with the principles of interpretation: the total absence of definitions, explanations, examples, and context. This can be done with every one of the remaining alleged general skeptics: all those Greek Skeptics we haven't dealt with in detail (Timon of Phlius, Arcesilaus of Pitane, Carneades of Cyrene, Aenesidemus, and Agrippa), the Greek Sophists (Protagoras and Gorgias),[37] and then Democritus, Leucippus, and Xenophanes.

My general conclusion, then, is that in the case of Sextus (the only supposed skeptic for whom there is a mass of primary data) there is overwhelming reason to believe that he is not a general skeptic, and that in the case of all the rest there is woefully insufficient reason to believe that any of them is. This amounts to saying that thesis 7—the existence thesis about general skeptics—is either false or is unwarranted by the evidence; and that implies that thesis 3—the genetic thesis about the conditions under which epistemology and its problems arise (e.g., Russell, Ayer, Hamlyn, Quine, and Pollock)—is false, or is at any rate unwarranted by the evidence.

2.2 Plato, Epistemology, and General Skepticism: The Historical Thesis (Thesis 5) and the Genetic Thesis (Thesis 3) Revisited

2.2.1 My interest in the historical thesis is due exclusively to its alleged link with the genetic thesis (that Plato originated epistemology in response to the general skepticism of the Sophists). However, at least one major philosophical historian of pre-Socratic and early Greek philosophy does not subscribe to the historical thesis: according to Jonathan Barnes, epistemology was invented by the early pre-Socratics, centuries before Plato.[38] I am myself prepared to acknowledge that Plato, if anyone, was the true originator of epistemology (at least in the sense specified by Guthrie and Hamlyn) and that he originated it in the *Theaetetus*. But given what at bottom is at stake—the very conception of epistemology, and more generally of philosophy, with all the massive implications of such determinations about matters of the most fundamental and general human concern—it must be said that the notion of the founder, inventor, or originator of a discipline, especially of one as controversial as epistemology (and more generally of philosophy), is too amorphous to sustain objective investigation and resolution of disagreements such as that between Russell, Guthrie, Hamlyn, and company and Barnes. Especially where such disciplines are concerned, there are no generally accepted criteria of the notion of originator, or any criteria at all, for that matter. Thus it is that, depending in part upon the subjective inclinations of scholars, Aristotle is singled out as the founder of metaphysics (Collingwood), although centuries earlier Parmenides engaged in recognizably metaphysical speculation; Aristotle again as the founder of logic (Bochenski), or Leibniz instead (C. I. Lewis), although recognizably logical speculations are to be found earlier than Leibniz *or* Aristotle.

2.2.2 If we take for granted the conception of epistemology with which Guthrie, Hamlyn, and company operate, it is undeniable that Plato is the originator of epistemology. But if Barnes had taken the conception for granted, he would have come to the same conclusion: there is just one philosopher—Plato—who first satisfies their criteria. But that conclusion exposes the unacceptability of their conception of epistemology. The epistemological enterprise is not, except arbitrarily, to be confined to the investigation, more or less methodical and systematic, of the questions these philosophers identify as basic for epistemology. Epistemological inquiries and speculations can go on and have gone on in the absence of the epistemological enterprise as conceived in terms of those basic questions. Philosophers universally recognized as epistemologists (recognized in fact by Russell, Guthrie, Hamlyn, and others)[39] have engaged in it without dealing with their basic questions, especially with the question which they identify as the most basic: "What is the nature of knowledge?" It suffices to cite Hume: in the *Treatise* and *Enquiries* his treatment of the concept of knowledge is at best perfunctory and derivative, nowhere approaching that of Plato, nowhere making knowledge itself the main or even a considerable subject of investigation, and nowhere engaging in a search for the essence of knowledge. By the Guthrie-Hamlyn criteria, Hume is not an epistemologist at all. But Hume *is* an epistemologist, and so it is the criteria which are too restrictive and thus inadequate.

This shows that it is possible to engage in recognizably epistemological inquiry and speculation that is not confined to the questions or pursued in the ways specified by Guthrie, Hamlyn, and company. As Parmenides engaged in metaphysical speculation, despite the unquestionable preeminence in some sense of Aristotle, so too did many of the pre-Socratic philosophers engage in epistemological inquiry and speculation, despite the acknowledged preeminence (again unquestionable) of Plato and the unprecedented character of his epistemological inquiries in the *Theaetetus*. But these two features of Plato's epistemological investigations, although relevant to some questions, are irrelevant to the most basic, which is whether epistemology in the sense of epistemological inquiries and speculations, not in the arbitrary sense laid down by Hamlyn and Guthrie, arose in response to general skepticism. My answer to that basic question is that there is no evidence in the surviving literature of any of these pre-Socratic or pre-Platonic philosophers (the so-called fragments) that their epistemological inquiries and speculations arose in response to general skepticism.[40]

2.2.3 There is, furthermore, no evidence in the Platonic dialogues that Plato's epistemological investigations, even in the *Theaetetus* (the locus, according to Guthrie, Hamlyn, and company, of Plato's invention of epistemology), arose in response to general skepticism, and conclusive evidence that it did not. In the *Theaetetus,* Plato begins (after the usual preparatory introduction) by having Socrates say (145B) that he cannot make out what knowledge is; and very soon, after some fumbling misstarts, Theaetetus proposes the theory that knowledge (*epistēmē*) is perception (*aisthēsis*). It is one of three theories of knowledge advanced and critically examined in the dialogue, the second being that knowledge is true opinion (*alēthēs doxa* [187B]) and the third being that knowledge is true opinion accompanied by an account (*logos* [201C]). But even these meager data suffice to show that in the very dialogue in which Plato is supposed to have founded or originated epistemology, which up to that point is supposed to have been nonexistent (like the non-Euclidean geometries invented by Gauss, Bolyai, Lobachevsky, and Riemann), Plato begins at the very outset by considering a theory of knowledge—a central component of any complete epistemology—that existed before he began to consider it. The same is true of the remaining two theories of knowledge, none of which was ever held by Plato or Socrates, and the third of which is expressly ascribed by Theaetetus (201C) to someone unnamed who, having made the distinction between knowledge and true judgment or opinion, also advanced just this theory that knowledge is true judgment plus an account (or explanation, or reason: in short, justification). Something very like the first theory is traceable to Heraclitus: not that knowledge *is* perception but that it is obtainable by perception (fragments 55, 101a, and 107).

It is true that shortly after Theaetetus advances the first theory—in response not to general skepticism but to Socrates' questions—Socrates proceeds to identify the theory with various statements of Protagoras: first that man is the measure of all things, and so on, and then that any given thing *is* to one perceiver of it whatever it *appears* to that perceiver to be and is to a second perceiver whatever it appears to the second to be, "appearing" (*phantasia*) then being interpreted by Socrates to mean "perceiving" (152C). Subsequently combining Theaetetus' first theory of knowledge, construed in such quasi-Protagorean terms (for which there is in fact no known historical justification), with a Cratylus-like extreme version of Heraclitean doctrine to the effect that everything is always changing (152C–153D), Socrates then argues that this composite doctrine (never held by anyone) has two absurd and intolerable consequences: first, that knowledge is impossible; second, that all discourse is impossible (179C–183D). Here at last is the thesis of general skepticism—concocted by "interpretation" and ascribable to nobody—that our own contemporaries have made so much of in their conceptions of epistemology and of its proper functions. Plato-Socrates then proceeds to subject the composite doctrine and its consequences to severe criticism.

But Plato's epistemological opposition to general skepticism, which is undeniable, is one thing; the question of what prompted his epistemological investigations is another. My thesis is that there is no evidence in the *Theaetetus* or in any of his other dialogues that they arose in response to general skepticism. The first theory of knowledge advanced in the *Theaetetus* is advanced not in response to general skepticism (of which there is no trace at that point or earlier in the dialogue) but in response to a series of questions put by Socrates to Theaetetus: first, which of the young men of Athens are thought likely to attain distinction? (143C); second, is Theaetetus learning astronomy and the other subjects from Theodorus? (145C); third, does learning about something mean becoming wiser about it? (145D); fourth, is wisdom in any way different from knowledge? (145D); and finally, after Theaetetus has answered the fourth question by saying that wisdom and knowledge are the same thing, Socrates' expression of puzzlement— "That is precisely what I am puzzled about. I cannot make out to my own satisfaction what knowledge is" (145E). Shortly thereafter, as noted above, the first theory of knowledge is elicited under the stimulus of further Socratic questioning. The question of general skepticism does not even arise in the dialogue until the first theory of knowledge has been elicited by means of other, wholly nonskeptical questions; and the question does not arise at all in connection with the second and third theories of knowledge.

2.2.4 There is not only no evidence in the *Theaetetus* that its epistemological investigations were engendered or prompted (Quine's term) by general skepticism; there is evidence elsewhere in the dialogues—in my judgment conclusive evidence—that Plato's epistemological investigations were not so engendered. There is a consensus among contemporary Plato scholars that Plato's dialogues fall into chronological groupings designated as early, middle, and late. There is also a consensus that the central focus of the early group of dialogues is moral-ethical; of the middle group, metaphysical; and of the late group, ontological and epistemological.[41] The *Theaetetus,* it is generally agreed, falls into the late group. If, then, there are dialogues that are earlier than the *Theaetetus* and that engage in epistemological inquiry without being prompted by or arising in response to general skepticism (whether that of the Sophists or of any of the pre-Socratics, none of whom, according to my investigation in 2.1, is a general skeptic), there is evidence, and conclusive evidence, that Plato's epistemological investigations, like those of all classical epistemologists (from Parmenides to Chisholm), arose in response to other considerations which are largely if not wholly nonskeptical in nature (for which see section 3.2). There are in fact at least six such dialogues: the *Meno,* the *Phaedo,* the *Republic,* the *Symposium,* and the *Phaedrus,* all of which belong to the middle period, and the *Charmides,* in the early period. All contain investigations of the concept of knowledge (although none to the extent that the *Theaetetus* and the *Sophist* do), but none does so in response to general skepticism or, indeed, skepticism of any kind.

Having concluded in section 2.1 that the existence thesis and the genetic thesis are false, I now find my conclusion reinforced by this examination of Plato. To that conclusion, therefore, I now add the conclusion that the historical thesis, too, is false.

2.3 An Analytic Theory of Knowledge in the Context of an Analytic Theory of Epistemology: Thesis 2 and Thesis 1

2.3.1 Roderick Chisholm has posed two fundamental questions of epistemology: "*What* do we know—in other words, what is the *extent* of our knowledge? And how are we to decide, in any particular case, *whether* we know—in other words, what are the *criteria* of knowing?"[42] My question is: Is it possible for a philosopher who subscribes to an analytic theory of knowledge in the context of an analytic theory of epistemology to answer those questions, and if so, how? Hamlyn, for one, endorses the idea of a complete epistemology;[43] but what he understands by the idea neither he nor any other adherent of analytic epistemology defines or explains. Nevertheless, he does two things that make it possible to determine what he takes a complete epistemology to be. He defines epistemology as "that branch of philosophy which is concerned with the nature and scope of knowledge, its presuppositions and basis, and the general reliability of claims to knowledge" ("Epistemology," 8–9);[44] and in more or less general terms he lays out the philosophical problems about knowledge as those concerned with the nature and general conditions of knowledge, the scope of knowledge, and special disciplines and fields of knowledge (e.g., science, mathematics, history, and religion; whence philosophy of science, of mathematics, of history, and of religion [*Theory of Knowledge*, 3–7, esp. 7]). A complete epistemology, then, would presumably be one that deals with all the essential problems of epistemology indicated in the definition of epistemology and specified in general terms in the account of the philosophical problems about knowledge. It would seem, then, that Hamlyn's reference to the scope of knowledge is the equivalent of Chisholm's reference to the extent of knowledge, and that Hamlyn's reference to the general reliability of claims to knowledge is the equivalent of Chisholm's reference to the decision problem. In *The Theory of Knowledge*, the whole of part 1 ("The Conditions of Knowledge") is concerned to establish the possibility of knowledge-in-general in opposition to general skepticism, and the whole of part 2 ("The Scope of Knowledge") is concerned to establish the possibility of knowledge-in-special ("whole ranges of forms of knowledge" [6]; knowledge by perception, knowledge by memory, knowledge of oneself and others, and a priori knowledge, respectively in chaps. 6, 7, 8, and 9) in opposition to the limited skepticisms with respect to perception and so forth.

2.3.2 I can best answer my question—I show in section 3.1 how Chisholm answers his own questions—if I first set forth an account of a complete epistemology as it is conceived in the classical world tradition.[45] Epistemology so conceived (e.g., by Locke or Descartes) is designed to answer Chisholm's two questions among others; and so classical epistemologists set up a fundamental desideratum that guides the whole epistemological enterprise—that of providing a general critique of the grounds upon which any knowledge-claim may be justified or refuted. In order to do this, classical epistemologists formulate a system of principles by means of which any cognitive claim—whether a claim with respect to the formal validity of any argument or with respect to the logical truth or empirical truth of any other sort of statement—can rationally be assessed. In order to carry out such a rational assessment, conceptual clarification of the terms of epistemic judgment is required, and the principles of assessment must themselves be justified. Thus, a complete epistemology so conceived is in part desiderative (setting out the general purposes of the epistemological enterprise), in part normative (setting out the general principles by means of which to determine the cognitive merit of any cognitive claim), in part analytic (formulating the conceptual apparatus of epistemology), and in part descriptive or metaphysical (providing an account of man's cognitive powers: perceptual, memorial, rational, intuitional, etc.).

Logic classically conceived (from Aristotle to Quine) is thus a part of epistemology thus comprehensively conceived. The fundamental desideratum of logicians in the classical tradition is the more limited one of the assessment of the formal validity of any argument and the logical truth of any statement. In order to carry out that task, classical logicians formulate general normative principles of formal validity and of logical truth (a truth-functional argument is valid if and only if . . . ; a truth-functional sentence is logically true if and only if . . . ; and so on); analyze or devise terms of logical appraisal (definitions of truth-functional connectives and of logical validity, implication, equivalence, and so on); analyze decision procedures (for deciding, given any argument, whether it is valid, etc., or not) and of proof procedures (for determining, given any argument, that its conclusion is formally derivable from its premises if in fact the conclusion is derivable, or, given any premises, what conclusions are formally derivable from them); and formulate principles and procedures for paraphrasing arguments and statements couched in ordinary or extraordinary (e.g., scientific, metaphysical, religious, or theological) language into logical form and then reducing these logical paraphrases to logical schemata, to which the formal techniques of logic are then applicable. So when logicians speak of the scope of logic in general, or of the scope of its branches (truth-functional, syllogistic, monadic-quantificational, general-quantificational, identity), they are speaking of its general power to assess *any* argument (as formally valid or invalid) or *any* statement (as true by virtue of its logical form, or not).[46]

That is how the scope of classical epistemology too (sufficiently developed, of course) is conceived: in terms of its capacity, when applied, to assess the cognitive merit of any knowledge-claim framed in the form of an argument or inference or statement purporting to be true by virtue of its logical form or in virtue of the facts of reality. As classical logicians provide or attempt to provide an answer to Chisholm's two questions in terms of logical matters ("What do we know *logically*—in other words, what is the extent of our *logical* knowledge? And how are we to decide, in any particular case of a claim to logical knowledge, *whether* we know—in other words, what are the criteria of *logical* knowledge?"), so classical epistemologists provide or attempt to provide an answer to those questions in terms of *all* matters, logical and nonlogical alike. That is precisely what the applicability and so the utility of logic consists in, and that is precisely what the applicability and so the utility of epistemology consists in. If the principles of logic were inapplicable to actual arguments and statements for the purpose of assessing the merit of the cognitive claims made in terms of them, it would have no utility at all; and if the principles of epistemology were inapplicable to actual knowledge-claims (e.g., knowledge-claims about the existence and nature of God, of microscopic and macroscopic entities, in the present, in the past, or in the future, of moral and spiritual questions, of political, social, and economic questions, and so on), epistemology too would have no utility at all. Its capacity to apply to all actual and possible knowledge-claims is precisely what a complete epistemology is, according to the classical conception of epistemology, whether they be the claims of common sense, science, religion, theology, astrology, or whatever. The knowledge-claims of philosophers themselves—whether moral, metaphysical, or epistemological philosophers—fall under the jurisdiction of a complete epistemology; and so do knowledge-claims about the very nature of epistemology—for example, the claim that epistemology is to be defined and/or otherwise explained in terms of general skepticism.

2.3.3 The idea, engendered by Hamlyn's definition of epistemology, that his conception of epistemology is traditional[47] is soon dispelled by his pervasive critique of "traditional" epistemology: his repudiation of what he takes to be its distinctive features—its taking for granted the nature of knowledge, its seeking instead to establish unshakeable foundations of knowledge by discovering certainties, indubitables, or infallibilities, its attempts to counter general skepticism either by rationalist methods (Descartes) or by empiricist methods (Locke), its architectural model of the structure of knowledge, and so on (Hamlyn, *Theory of Knowledge,* chap. 2). In fact, however, his repudiation of the traditional or classical conception of epistemology is more radical than he himself makes it out to be or, indeed, seems even to realize. When in his definition of epistemology he makes reference to the general reliability of knowledge-claims, it is natural to take him to mean what classical epistemologists mean—for example, Chisholm in his reference to the decision problem. And when in Hamlyn's account of the scope of a complete epistemology he makes reference to the scope of knowledge, it is natural to take him to mean what classical epistemologists mean—for example, Chisholm in his reference to the extent of our knowledge ("extent" being a term which Hamlyn in fact uses in the very first sentence of the first chapter of his book, clearly using it as a synonym of "scope")—or what classical logicians mean when they speak of the scope of logic or of logical knowledge.

But Hamlyn does not mean by "the scope of knowledge" what Chisholm means by "the extent of knowledge."[48] Hamlyn's account of the scope of knowledge is not an answer to Chisholm's question, "*What* do we know—in other words, what is the *extent* of our knowledge?"; and Hamlyn's account of the general reliability of claims to knowledge is not an answer to Chisholm's question, "How are we to decide, in any particular case, *whether* we know—in other words, what are the *criteria* of knowing?" This failure is no accident or matter of oversight; it is a matter of principle: it follows from the very conception of epistemology adopted by Hamlyn and all analytic epistemologists. Let us see how and why this is so.

2.3.4 In the first sentence of the following passage we have Hamlyn's theory of knowledge; the rest of the passage explains it:

> One might say, in sum, that someone knows that *p* if he is in the appropriate position to certify or give his authority to the truth of *p*. Someone will be in this position if one or more of a number of relevant considerations do not rule it out. The considerations mentioned thus furnish necessary conditions of knowledge. . . . These two conditions—truth and belief in it—are positive, but other necessary conditions of knowledge—or some of them, at any rate—are negative in form. The man who knows must *not* be guessing, he must *not* hit on the truth by chance, he must *not* rely on bad reasons if he relies on reasons at all. It is the fact that these conditions are negative that makes it impossible to give the sufficient conditions of knowledge except in a vague and general formula of the kind that I have invoked. (*Theory of Knowledge*, 101)

But how is the theory to be used? What use can be made of it for the purpose of answering Chisholm's or Hamlyn's question about the scope of knowledge? And how with its help are we to decide, in any particular case, *whether* we know?

Consider standard procedure in logic when we are confronted, say, by a particular argument or particular statement, and the question is how we are to decide in the case of this particular argument whether it is logically valid, or in the case of the particular statement whether it is logically true. The typical procedure in logic is first to formulate a definition of logical validity or of logical truth. But such definitions by themselves are insufficient for the purpose; they have to be supplemented by a number of other elements of the total logical apparatus: first by the techniques of logical paraphrase (putting the original argument into logical form) and logical schematization (reducing the argument, now logically paraphrased, into abstract schematic form) and then by decision procedures and proof procedures. Without putting the original argument through the processes of logical paraphrase and logical schematization and then applying the appropriate decision procedures or proof procedures (this whole process being fully described in, e.g., Quine's *Methods of Logic* or in any comparable text), the original argument's logical validity cannot be assessed (except intuitively).

So it is with Hamlyn's (or, for that matter, anyone's) theory of knowledge: by itself, unsupplemented, it is insufficient for the purpose of answering Chisholm's question how we are to decide, with respect to any particular *p*, whether we know *p*. How, then, does Hamlyn supplement it? In fact in no way: supplementation of it by means of procedures or criteria which would enable anyone to determine, with respect to any particular *p*, that we know or do not know *p*, forms no part of his "complete epistemology." When he initially explains his use of the expression "the scope of knowledge," he explains it by the expression "what it is that in general deserves the title of knowledge" and immediately adds:

> I say "in general" because the problems that confront the philosopher here are not the specific ones of whether any particular claims made by a scientist, an historian, or a specialist within any other discipline deserve the name of knowledge. The verdict on such claims can be arrived at only by those with the relevant specialist knowledge, or by those who have the techniques or knowledge of the methodology appropriate for the discovery of the truth in question. The same is true even of particular claims to knowledge made by the man in the street; for only those who have access to the relevant facts, who can make the relevant inferences, and so on, are competent to pass judgment on such claims. (*Theory of Knowledge*, 4)

What, then, according to Hamlyn, is it that the nontraditional or new epistemologist is investigating when he investigates and seeks to determine the scope of knowledge? He says that an account of the nature of knowledge may have further implications for further problems concerning the scope of knowledge (*Theory of Knowledge, 4*);[49] but theory of knowledge *is* an account of the nature of knowledge (9), and according to Hamlyn a correct account of the nature of knowledge may serve to counter skepticism of the general and limited varieties by depriving them of any justification. Thus, when Hamlyn seeks to determine the scope of knowledge, all he seeks to determine is the *possibility* of knowledge-in-general, in opposition to the general skeptic who says that knowledge-in-general is impossible, and the *possibility* of knowledge-in-special (knowledge by perception, by memory, etc.), in opposition to the limited skeptic who maintains that such knowledge is impossible. Establishment of the possibility of knowledge-in-general is the central burden of part 1 of his *Theory of Knowledge,* and establishment of the possibility of knowledge-in-special ("the problem of whether whole ranges of forms of knowledge are possible, and if so, how," as he puts it [6]; see also chap. 10) is the major burden of part 2 of the book.

This retreat from a concern with Chisholm's first question explains the unconcern with Chisholm's second question. Neither Hamlyn nor Ayer nor any other analytic epistemologist has any interest in determining the actual scope of human knowledge in Chisholm's sense, and so as a consequence attempts no answer to Chisholm's question about the criteria of knowing, in the sense in which criteria are relevant to the question of deciding, with respect to any particular p, whether we know p. Hamlyn says as much in so many words; and Danto says that a theory of truth does not augment the stock of truths any more than a theory of knowledge increases the stock of knowledge. What in analytic epistemology has replaced the concern with Chisholm's and the classical epistemologist's two fundamental questions is the obsession with philosophical skepticism of the general and limited kinds: "the theory of knowledge is primarily an exercise in scepticism; the advancement and attempted rebuttal of arguments which are intended to prove that we do not know what we think we know."[50] That is why in Hamlyn's "complete" epistemology his theory of knowledge is unsupplemented by any measures that make it possible to answer Chisholm's and the classical epistemologist's questions about the extent of our knowledge and about the criteria of knowing.

Of course, a theory of knowledge, as such, does not by itself enable us to determine the scope or extent of knowledge or to decide, with respect to any particular p, whether we know p. But a logical theory of validity, implication, equivalence, or inference is in exactly the same boat: definitions of logical validity, logical truth, and all the rest have to be supplemented by all the paraphernalia already specified if any particular argument or statement is to be determined to be logically valid or logically true. But given all that supplementary paraphernalia, logic *does* make it possible to decide, with respect to any particular argument or statement, whether it is what we think it is. Hamlyn's exemption of the particular knowledge-claims of scientists and other specialists from the investigations of epistemologists has no counterpart in logic, which after all is a branch of epistemology. The logician does not ask whether the particular arguments or statements he intends to assess were claimed to be logically valid or logically true by scientists, historians, theologians, astrologists, and the like; he assesses them anyway. He does not care whether the particular claims to logical knowledge are made by the man in the street or the man in the moon: the origin of the claims is irrelevant. And contrary to what Danto says, a theory of logical inference, when supplemented by all the paraphernalia specified, *does* augment, or at any rate is in principle capable of augmenting, the stock of logical inferences known to be sound; and a theory of logical knowledge *does* increase, or at any rate is in principle capable of increasing, the scope of our logical knowledge. The collection of actual logical inferences identified by twentieth-century logicians as logically valid—a collection which has been increasing since Aristotle's time—is vastly greater than the collection identified by Aristotle as logically valid. All this is common knowledge among logicians, and I assume I do not need to provide a list of logically sound inferences known to contemporaries which were unknown to Aristotle, and which were in fact discovered with the help of logical techniques (decision procedures and proof procedures) unknown to Aristotle.

After propounding his moral philosophy, Ayer explains what he has done in the following terms:

> The theory is entirely on the level of analysis; it is an attempt to show what people are doing when they make moral judgments; it is not a set of suggestions as to what moral judgments they are to make. And this is true of all moral philosophy, as I understand it. All moral theories . . ., in so far as they are philosophical theories, are neutral as regards actual conduct. To speak technically, they belong to the field of meta-ethics, not ethics proper.[51]

What this implies is that a moral theory "neutral" in this sense is in principle incapable of answering Chisholm's question "How are we to decide, in any particular case, whether or not a given act is right?"[52] which is the analogue for moral philosophy of his question "How are we to decide, in the case of any particular p, whether or not we know that p?" Thus it is that a theory of knowledge and a theory of epistemology like that of Hamlyn, Ayer, and Danto, which is "neutral" in the same sense, is in principle inapplicable to particular cases, and so is useless. Like Russell's possibilist conception of philosophy, this is a possibilist conception of knowledge and of epistemology: at best it can tell us that knowledge-in-general is possible and that "whole ranges of forms of knowledge are possible," but never what is in fact the case.

3

Epistemology, Philosophy, and the Nature of Man

3.1 A Classical Theory of Knowledge in the Context of a Classical Theory of Epistemology

3.1.1 SINCE 1957, RODERICK CHISHOLM—WHOSE EPISTEMOLOGICAL INVESTI-gations are for their depth, breadth, and sustained development unequaled in the twentieth century—has attempted to provide what constitutes, according to the classical conception of epistemology, "a complete epistemology."[1] Although he does not use that term or any equivalent, and although he also does not say that he subscribes to the classical theory of epistemology (which he never mentions), the slow but steady development of his epistemological views has in fact moved toward the realization of that conception. This fact has been obscured by two other facts: first, Chisholm himself has never claimed the development of a complete epistemology in the classical sense as an overriding desideratum; and second, although every aspect of Chisholm's epistemology has for thirty years been the subject of intense critical scrutiny—for example, his theory of knowl-edge, his theory of perceiving, his theory of sensing, his foundationalism, and his analysis of numerous epistemic concepts—the general character of his general epistemology has been ignored or overlooked.[2]

No one, including Chisholm himself, it seems, has viewed his work as a whole. Nevertheless, his epistemology is a complete epistemology (at least in principle, or potentially, not yet being complet*ed*) in the classical sense: Chisholm sub-scribes to the general desideratum of the classical conception of epistemology; he provides a general system of general normative principles of knowledge and reasonable belief; he advances justification of that general system and those general principles; he carries out a full conceptual analysis embodied in a system of definitions of epistemic terms; and he provides an account (although so far only summarily and schematically) of the cognitive powers of man which are presupposed by the general normative principles of knowledge and reasonable belief. Important (even if eventually judged to be unsound) as the specific elements of his general epistemology may be, far more fundamental and significant, for my purposes, are these general features of his general epistemology themselves: its completeness (which is not that of Hamlyn) in terms of the classical conception of epistemology, which distinguishes his work from that of every other twentieth-century epistemologist known to me.

3.1.2 In epistemology, Chisholm has developed a system of epistemic logic.[3] Like any system of formal logic intended to be applicable to arguments and statements couched in ordinary or extraordinary language (e.g., Quine's *Methods of Logic*), it has at least two parts or dimensions: the conceptual and the procedural. The conceptual dimension he explains summarily in the following terms:

> We have been trying to explicate some of the basic concepts of the theory of knowledge. It is obvious that, if we are able to explicate any given concept, we can do so only by making use of certain other concepts. Or, to put the matter in a somewhat different way, if we are able to define any given expression, we can do so only by making use of other expressions that we do not define. We have been using the undefined technical term, "*p* is more reasonable than *q* for *S* at *t*."[4]

Like the formal logician who unavoidably takes some truth-functional connective or connectives as basic and undefined, and then defines others in terms of it, and so on, Chisholm takes the expression, "*p* is more reasonable than *q* for *S* at *T*" as basic, and then defines "*h* is *beyond reasonable doubt* for *S*" in terms of it; then in succession, in a chain of connected definitions, defines "*h* has *some presumption in its favor* for *S*"; "*h* is *acceptable* for *S*"; "*h* is *certain* for *S*"; "*h* is *evident* for *S*"; and so on for a list of thirty-one definitions of epistemic concepts (*Theory of Knowledge,* 135–38; the volume's appendix lists these definitions in order).

But these definitions, like the corresponding definitions of logical concepts, are inapplicable and therefore unusable without provision of a procedural apparatus. The procedural dimension he explains summarily in the following terms:

> The things that we ordinarily say we *know* are not things that are thus "directly evident." But in justifying the claim to know any particular one of these things, we can be led back, in the manner described, to various things that *are* directly evident. Should we say, therefore, that the whole of what we know, at any given time, is a kind of "structure" having its "foundation" in what happens to be directly evident at that time? If we do say this, then we should be prepared to say just how it is that the foundation serves to support the rest of the structure. But this question is difficult to answer, for the support that the foundation gives would seem to be neither deductive nor inductive. That is to say, it is not the kind of support that the premises of a deductive argument give to their conclusion, nor is it the kind of support that the premises of an inductive argument give to their conclusion. For if we take as our premises the whole of what is directly evident at any time, and if we make use of

no additional premises, then we cannot formulate a good deductive argument, and we cannot formulate a good inductive argument, in which any of the things we ordinarily say we know appears as a conclusion. It may be, therefore, that in addition to the "rules of deduction" and the "rules of induction," there are also certain basic "rules of evidence." The deductive logician tries to formulate the first type of rule; the inductive logician tries to formulate the second; and the epistemologist tries to formulate the third. (*Theory of Knowledge,* 2 – 3)

Underlying these rules of evidence is a theory of evidence, which he summarily explains in the following terms:

In investigating the theory of evidence from a philosopical—or Socratic—point of view, we make three general presuppositions.

We presuppose, first, that there *is* something that we know. . . . We presuppose, second, that the things we know are justified for us. . . . And we presuppose, third, that if we do thus have grounds or reasons for the things we think we know, then there are valid general principles of evidence—principles stating the general conditions under which we may be said to have grounds or reasons for what we believe. (*Theory of Knowledge,* 16–17)

He gives illustrative examples of such abstract rules of evidence: " 'What justifies me in believing that I know that *a* is *F* is the fact that it is evident to me that *b* is *G'* " (*Theory of Knowledge,* 18). For a concrete instance of such an abstract principle: " 'What justifies me in thinking I know that he has that disorder is the fact that it is evident to me that he has those symptoms' " (18). Presupposed by the answer just given, according to Chisholm, is an epistemic principle, or a rule of evidence, of the form " 'If it is evident to me that *b* is *G*, then it is evident to me that *a* is *F'* " *(19)*. Chisholm then formulates a series of Rules of Evidence, A to I:

(A) *S*'s being *F* is such that, if it occurs, then it is self-presenting to *S* that he is *F*.

(B) For any subject *S*, if *S* believes, without ground for doubt, that he is perceiving something to be *F*, then it is beyond reasonable doubt for *S* that he perceives something to be *F*.

(C) For any subject *S*, if *S* believes, without ground for doubt, that he is perceiving something to be *F*, then it is evident for *S* that he perceives something to be *F*. (73,76,78)

Then come a number of principles of evidence concerning memory (80–81), confirmation, and concurrence (82 – 83); "and finally, from our concurrent set of propositions—now reasonable as well as acceptable—we extract still another class of propositions; . . . countenanced as evident":

(I) If *S* believes, without ground for doubt, that he perceives something to be *F*, and if the proposition that there is something that is *F* is a member of a set of concurrent propositions each of which is beyond reasonable doubt for *S*, then it is evident for *S* that he perceives something to be *F*.

How Chisholm arrives at all these definitions of epistemic concepts and formulations of these principles of evidence is not here my concern. It may well be that some or even all of his definitions are unacceptable or incorrect and that some or even all of his principles of evidence are unacceptable or inadequate; and that too is not my concern here. What is my concern here is what he next says: "The set of concurrent propositions cited just above [not included in the passages I have quoted] includes the perceptual proposition 'A cat is on the roof.' Hence, in virtue of the principle *I*, and the definition of knowledge to be proposed in Chapter 6, we may be able to say, at last, that *S* knows that there is a cat on the roof." (84). The definition of knowledge proposed in chapter 6 is as follows:

D6.4 *h* is *known* by *S* = Df *h* is accepted by *S*; *h* is true; and *h* is nondefectively evident for *S*. (110)

Chisholm has thus provided what, it seems to be, is necessary if a "theory of knowledge," or an epistemology, is to be both applicable and useful: a conceptual apparatus (the definitions of the epistemic concepts, etc.) and a procedural apparatus (the principles of evidence). Chisholm provides definitions of *beyond reasonable doubt* (D1.1), *some presumption in its favor* (D1.2), *acceptable* (D1.3), *certain* (D1.4), *evident* (D1.5), and so on, for thirty-one definitions altogether. But the definition of *knowledge*, of *h is known by S*, taken by itself, is inapplicable and therefore useless; taken in conjunction with any or all of the remaining thirty definitions of epistemic concepts, it is no less inapplicable and therefore useless. The definition of knowledge and likewise of these other epistemic concepts, becomes applicable and usable for the purpose of determining the rational justifiability of any given or possible claim to knowledge only when it is combined, as in principle it is combined in Chisholm's system of epistemic logic, with the principles of evidence. It is in these terms that Chisholm *can* answer the two fundamental questions of classical epistemology which Hamlyn and all those whose epistemology is confined to the analysis of epistemic terms and statements cannot answer: "*What* do we know? or, What is the *extent* of our knowledge? and How are we to decide, in any particular case, *whether* we know? or, What are the *criteria* of knowing?"

3.2 A Classical Theory of Epistemology
in the Context of a Classical Theory of Philosophy

3.2.1 After this lengthy examination of the new epistemology it is time to summarize it before setting forth my concluding views. Having in Chapter 1 summarily explained the new epistemology in its more general analytic context (sections 1.1 and 1.2), I then set forth its scope thesis (section 1.3) and its existence thesis (section 1.4) at length. In Chapter 2, I examined first the existence thesis and the genetic thesis (section 2.1) at length, concluding that both were false or unwarranted by the available evidence; then the historical thesis (section 2.2), concluding that it too was false, or unwarranted by the available evidence; then the definitional thesis concerning knowledge and the scope theses concerning both the scope of epistemology and the scope of knowledge (section 2.3), concluding that the definitional thesis, being inapplicable, was useless, that the scope thesis concerning knowledge was incapable of providing what it seemed to promise, and that the scope thesis concerning epistemology was arbitrary and unjustifiable.

3.2.2 This leaves thesis (1), the definitional thesis concerning the nature of epistemology itself, which I have yet to assess. That thesis (although none of its numerous proponents has said so) has in fact two foundations. The narrower foundation consists of the compound thesis consisting of the existence thesis, the genetic thesis, and the historical thesis. But if my critique of these three pillars of the definitional theory of epistemology is correct, that foundation is nonexistent: all three theses are either false or are unwarranted by the available evidence. The definitional theory thus rests on no foundation, being suspended, so to speak, in midair. But these are the only specific positive grounds upon which the classical theory of epistemology can rationally be repudiated; there are no others. The broader, more generic foundation is the analytic theory (or theories) of philosophy itself; if philosophy itself is wholly analytic, then all its branches (ethics, metaphysics, and finally epistemology itself) are analytic, too. The conception of the branches of philosophy is derived from the conception of philosophy, the generic foundation of the whole enterprise as conceived in analytic philosophy. But that foundation itself is arbitrary, unwarranted by any evidence or other considerations, and, more fundamentally, unsound;[5] so that foundation, too, is not a foundation that is capable of supporting the conception of epistemology derived from it.

3.2.3 Every thesis of the new epistemology with which I have taken issue I have countered with a constructive or positive thesis of my own. My own historical thesis is indicated in the course of my critique of the new epistemology's historical thesis: there is evidence of epistemological inquiry and speculation almost from the very beginnings of Western philosophy and increasing evidence of increasing epistemological inquiry and speculation as the end of the pre-Socratic period is approached. Much of that evidence I have cited summarily, and all of it I can cite in detail if necessary. As for my existence thesis, it too has been indicated summarily in the course of my critique: none of the ancient philosophers is a general skeptic; all philosophers—ancient, medieval, modern, or contemporary—are limited skeptics. All philosophers in the history of philosophy, Eastern *or* Western, deny the possibility of knowledge with respect to some area of putative knowledge (because, e.g., there is nothing there to be known). For some Western philosophers, the area is theological; for others, mathematical; for others, astrological; for others, philosophical; for others, ethical; for others, metaphysical; for others, epistemological; for others, paranormal and extrasensory; for others, the past; and so on. And that is just as it should be, being little more than a corollary of what it is to be a philosopher, endlessly critical, questioning (not necessarily *doubting*), and probing; but not *just* so. On the contrary. But what I deny is what everyone else—for example, Ayer—asserts: that there is a special class of philosophers who may be justifiably classified as philosophical skeptics, all the rest being not so classifiable.

3.2.4 My "genetic" thesis has not been indicated heretofore; but because it seems to me that the terminology used by some ("arises against and by contrast with" [Hamlyn], "generate" [Pollock], "prompts" [Quine]) is misleading and even inaccurate, involving assumptions which themselves are false or unwarranted, I begin by reformulating the question: What, if any, are the conditions under which epistemological inquiry and speculation arise? I suggest that it is to be explained in two different ways by reference to two different sorts of conditions: conditions external and conditions internal. The first—the external conditions—is the existence of fundamental philosophical disagreements about matters of ultimate and general human concern: fundamental disagreements about questions moral (e.g., the existence and nature of the good, the right, and the obligatory), metaphysical (e.g., the nature and kinds of reality), religious (e.g., the existence and nature of God)—fundamental disagreements of all such kinds that in addition have shown themselves to be unresolvable by any rational means of a nonepistemological kind available to all those who find themselves entangled in such fundamental disagreements. An example of a fundamental metaphysical disagreement of this kind, to this day unresolved, is that between metaphysical monism (Parmenides) and metaphysical pluralism (Heraclitus); of a fundamental religious disagreement, to this day unresolved, that between theism and atheism; of a fundamental ethical disagreement, to this day unresolved, that between absolutism and relativism, or that between cognitivism and noncognitivism; and so on without end.

In such contexts, I suggest that the epistemological enterprise—reflection upon the questions whether we know, what we know, how we know, and so on—

arises when all other means of resolving these fundamental disagreements are found to fail. In such circumstances the question will inevitably arise why it is that men of good will and intellectual integrity are unable to resolve those fundamental disagreements despite seeming to be fully aware of the considerations underlying the disagreements.[6] Like two astronomers with their telescopes trained on the same region whose reports of the existence and character of the things to be found in that region are in fundamental conflict, each astronomer will inevitably wonder, to begin with, what is wrong with the telescope of his colleague, or even with his colleague, and then, more fundamentally, what is wrong with his own telescope, or with himself. (It is a notable and significant fact that there is no evidence of wonderment of the latter kind among the major analytic philosophers.) Questions of such kinds, when the disagreements are of the fundamental kind indicated, are epistemological questions; and the attempt to answer such questions, both critically and contructively, issues in epistemology. In that context, epistemological inquiry functions as the court of last appeal (and if not epistemology, then what?): the last possible means of resolving otherwise unresolvable fundamental disagreements. Thus arises that branch of philosophy known as epistemology: as a consequence of fundamental disagreement, a *two*-sided affair, it is to be noted; not as a consequence of general skepticism, which is a one-sided affair. The whole history of global philosophy, Western *and* Eastern, bears out this interpretation, I believe, of one of the major conditions under which the general enterprise of philosophy arises. Two examples, one drawn from modern Western epistemology and one drawn from ancient Western metaphysics, will have to suffice by way of evidence.

In *An Essay Concerning Human Understanding,* John Locke writes that "my purpose [is], to enquire into the original, certainty, and extent of human Knowledge, together with the grounds and degrees of Belief, Opinion, and Assent";[7] and in "The Epistle to the Reader" with which he prefaces that work he writes:

> Were it fit to trouble thee with the history of this Essay, I should tell thee that five or six friends meeting at my chamber, and discoursing on a subject very remote from this, found themselves quickly at a stand by the difficulties that rose on every side. After we had a while puzzled ourselves without coming any nearer a resolution of those doubts which perplexed us, it came into my thoughts, that we took a wrong course; and that, before we set ourselves upon enquiries of that nature, it was necessary to examine our own abilities, and see what objects our understandings were or were not fitted to deal with.

In a footnote to this passage, Pringle-Pattison explains, "According to a manuscript note in a copy of the *Essay* which belonged to James Tyrrell, one of the friends present at the meeting, the difficulties arose in discussing 'the principles of morality and revealed religion.' "[8] In other words, there was discussion of

fundamental questions of morality and religion; there were fundamental disagreements among the discussants; the disagreements were unresolvable by whatever
means the discussants had recourse to; and Locke as a consequence turned to an
inquiry which is identifiable as a general epistemological inquiry. That Locke's
epistemological inquiry did not arise against or even in response to general
philosophical skepticism is clear enough from his whole *Essay* and otherwise
from his whole philosophical outlook, but it is especially clear in the following
passage, in which he expresses his scorn of such skepticism:

> But yet, if after all this anyone will be so skeptical as to distrust his senses, and to
> affirm that all we see and hear, feel and taste, think and do, during our whole being,
> is but the series and deluding appearances of a long dream whereof there is no reality;
> and therefore will question the existence of all things or our knowledge of anything:
> I must desire him to consider, that if all be a dream, then he doth but dream that he
> makes the question; and so it is not much matter that a waking man should answer
> him.[9]

According to Aristotle, metaphysics too, in the sense of first philosophy, arose
in response to fundamental disagreements about the first principles of philosophy.
In his *Metaphysics*, he writes: "It is necessary, with a view to the science
which we are seeking [protê philosophia, 'first philosophy'], first to recount the
difficulties which should first be discussed. These concern all the divergent views
which are held about first principles."[10] Among the disagreements he cites are
those between the "Physical" philosophers of early Greek philosophy and the
Pythagoreans and Platonists. In short, "first philosophy" was born out of fundamental philosophical disagreement about first principles of philosophy and Aristotle's subsequent attempt to resolve those disagreements. The similarity to the
first passage from Locke is striking, and generally overlooked.

All the same, there is, it seems to me, a still deeper source for "reflection upon
the nature of knowledge" (Chisholm), and it has nothing to do with external
conditions, either the external conditions which the new epistemologists (Russell,
Ayer, Hamlyn, Pollock, Quine, Schlick, et al.) cite, or those which Aristotle and
Locke cite. That deeper source, I believe, is simply the nature of man: the natural
tendency of the human mind to wonder about, to inquire into, and to reflect upon
the nature, scope, and means of knowledge; to wonder about, to inquire into,
and to reflect upon the questions whether it knows, how it knows, how much it
knows, how much it can in principle know, and what it is to know at all.[11] "Man,"
Sextus Empiricus said, "is by nature a truth-loving animal" (L.i.27); "All men,"
Aristotle said, "desire by nature to know":[12] and all men, I would add, desire by
nature to know whether they know, how they know, how much they know, how
much they can know, and what it is to know.[13] The instinct for knowing is
inherent in all men; for knowing in the special way of doing science equally so;

for knowing in the way of doing epistemology equally so; and more generally for knowing in the way of doing philosophy. The tendency of the human mind to engage in epistemological reflection and inquiry is as natural as the tendency of the human mind to engage in philosophical reflection and inquiry in general, and as natural as looking, eating, drinking, breathing, sleeping, laughing, and thinking in general.[14] There is no need to look for external sources or conditions of the general philosophical enterprise or of the special epistemological one, and no justification for it, any more than there is any need to look for external sources or conditions of the general human activities of looking, eating, drinking, sleeping, and thinking. To seek the source or condition of epistemological reflection and inquiry, as of philosophical reflection and inquiry generally, in the accidental historical occurrence of general skepticism—even if, contrary to fact, it had occurred—seems to me to have a grave tendency to impoverish and trivialize such reflection and inquiry. To seek its source rather in the attempt to resolve otherwise unresolvable fundamental disagreements of ultimate and universal human (not just academic philosophical) concern, or even more deeply as the natural impulse of the human mind, seems to me to restore to philosophy its fundamental human significance and importance: a significance and importance philosophy has had for 2,500 years, until the advent of analytic philosophy.[15]

NOTES

NAME INDEX

SUBJECT INDEX

INDEX OF GREEK TERMS, PHRASES, AND
SENTENCES CITED AND/OR DISCUSSED

NOTES

1. The Problem: A General Introduction

1. The terms "epistemology" and "theory of knowledge" are widely used in the literature as synonyms. In this work they are used differently: "epistemology" for the whole field of philosophical inquiry into the nature, types, means, and scope of knowledge; "theory of knowledge" strictly for what it says—theory of (the nature of) knowledge, on a par with theory of (the nature of) truth, belief, and so forth. See section 3.2 for a fuller account of the nature of epistemology.

2. Bertrand Russell, *The Problems of Philosophy* (1912; reprint, London: Oxford University Press, 1959), 149–51.

3. Bertrand Russell, *An Outline of Philosophy* (London: George Allen & Unwin, 1927), 1. For similar explanations indistinguishably of epistemology and philosophy, see his *Our Knowledge of the External World as a Field for Scientific Method in Philosophy* (Chicago and London: Open Court, 1915), 63–67, and *An Inquiry into Meaning and Truth* (New York: Norton, 1940), 40, where he uses "theory of knowledge" and "epistemology" to designate what in the earlier works he used "philosophy" to designate.

In "Russell on the Foundations of Knowledge," in *The Philosophy of Bertrand Russell*, ed. P. A. Schilpp (Evanston and Chicago: Northwestern University Press, 1944), 423, R. M. Chisholm had already pointed out that Russell defines philosophy and epistemology indistinguishably in terms of methodological skepticism. At that time the conception had not been as widely adopted as it has since, and so it did not then have the significance for philosophy which it has acquired in the following decades. But it must also be said that at that time I failed to realize the significance of Chisholm's observation.

4. A. J. Ayer, *The Problem of Knowledge* (London: Macmillan, 1956), viii. The same conception is to be found in Ayer's *The Concept of a Person and Other Essays* (London: Macmillan, 1963), 31, and *The Central Questions of Philosophy* (New York: Morrow, 1975), 1, 63; it is suggested more amorphously in almost all the rest of his works.

5. D. W. Hamlyn, "Epistemology, History of," in *The Encyclopedia of Philosophy*, ed. Paul Edwards (New York: Macmillan and Free Press, 1967), 3:8–9. Hereafter cited in text as "Epistemology."

6. D. W. Hamlyn, *The Theory of Knowledge* (Garden City: Doubleday, Anchor, 1970; London: Macmillan, 1971), 7–8.

7. This mingled historico-genetic thesis has its counterpart in ethics: "If physical philosophy begins in wonder, ethics may be said to have begun in scepticism"; Alexander Grant, *The Ethics of Aristotle*, 4th ed., 2 vols. (London, 1885). The thesis is no truer in ethics than it is in epistemology. For the thesis in epistemology, see sections 2.1 (the genetic thesis) and 2.2 (the historical thesis). The human concern about morality and moral philosophy has no essential connections with moral skepticism.

In the most comprehensive and thorough critique of ethical skepticism known to me, Panayot Butcharov still finds it possible to explain ethics itself in constructive and skeptical terms; see his *Skepticism in Ethics* (Bloomington: Indiana University Press, 1989), 29–30, 164–65.

8. W. V. Quine, "The Nature of Natural Knowledge," in *Mind and Language*, ed. Samuel Guttenplan (Oxford: Clarendon, 1975), 67–68. I owe thanks to Roger F. Gibson, Jr., for supplying me with this passage.

9. John L. Pollock, *Knowledge and Justification* (Princeton: Princeton University Press, 1974), 5. In his most recent major work in epistemology, Pollock still maintains many of the positions he advanced in his earlier work—for instance, that there are general philosophical skeptics and that these skeptics are insusceptible to rational considerations and so are best ignored; *Contemporary Theories of Knowledge* (Totowa: Rowman and Littlefield, 1986), 3–7.

10. Moritz Schlick, "The Foundations of Knowledge," and Hans Hahn, "Logic, Mathematics and Knowledge of Nature," both reprinted in *Logical Positivism*, A. J. Ayer ed. (Glencoe: Free Press, 1959), 209–27 and 146–66, respectively; Bertrand Russell, *A History of Western Philosophy* (New York: Simon and Schuster, 1945), 73. Neither Ayer nor Hamlyn nor Quine nor Pollock nor any of the others acknowledges Russell as the source of his conception of epistemology, apparently viewing it as a self-evident conception to which any epistemologist would subscribe.

11. W. K. C. Guthrie, *A History of Greek Philosophy*, 6 vols. (Cambridge: Cambridge University Press, 1962–81), 4:174, 5:65.

12. John Burnet, *Greek Philosophy: Thales to Plato* (1914; reprint, London: Macmillan, 1968), 9, 81, 157, 159; Russell, *A History of Western Philosophy*, 73; and Nicholas P. White, *Plato on Knowledge and Reality* (Indianapolis: Hackett, 1976), vi, 2, 147, 160, 217, and scattered throughout.

13. The significance of all this documentation emerges in section 1.4.

14. According to A. J. Ayer, himself one of the adherents of the new conception of philosophy, these conceptions are not new. The majority of the great figures in the history of philosophy were, according to him, analytic philosophers in his sense; *Language, Truth and Logic*, 2d ed. (London: Victor Gollancz, 1949, 51–56, esp. 52. That half a century later he still subscribes to this historical thesis is clear from his *Philosophy in the Twentieth Century* (New York: Random, Vintage, 1982), chap. 1, esp. 13–15.

For a very recent distortion of philosophy and its history, see A. C. Danto, "Philosophy and Its History," chap. 1 of *Connections to the World* (1989; New York: Harper & Row, Perennial Library, 1990), esp. 5.

15. Strictly speaking, neither Russell nor Moore was ever an adherent of the analytic conception of philosophy; both repeatedly repudiated it. But they are still widely so viewed, e.g., by Ayer, in *Logical Positivism*, and in *Philosophy in the Twentieth Century*, ix, where he writes of "what is loosely called the analytic movement, covering philosophers as diverse as Bertrand Russell, G. E. Moore, Ludwig Wittgenstein, Rudolf Carnap and other members of the Vienna Circle." That is like speaking of what is loosly called the school of logical positivism, covering philosophers as diverse as Parmenides, Pythagoras, Saint Augustine, and A. J. Ayer. It obliterates genuine, fundamental, and important cleavages to use classificatory schemes in that way. See note 23 to the present chapter and note 6 to chapter 2.

16. Bertrand Russell, *Mysticism and Logic and Other Essays* (London: Long, Green, 1918), 111–13; *Our Knowledge of the External World*, 33.

17. See John Passmore, "Philosophy," *Encyclopedia of Philosophy* 6:221.

18. Ludwig Wittgenstein, *Tractatus Logico-Philosophicus*, trans. D. F. Pears and B. F. McGuinness (London: Routledge & Kegan Paul, 1974), 4.0031; and see also 4.111–12; *Philosophical Investigations*, ed. G. E. M. Anscombe and R. Rhees, trans. G. E. M. Anscombe (Oxford: Basil Blackwell, 1953), 109, and see 119, 123, 124, 126, 127, 128, 133, 255.

19. Rudolf Carnap, *The Unity of Science* (London: Kegal Paul, Trench, Trubner, 1934), 21–22; *Philosophy and Logical Syntax* (London: Kegan Paul, Trench, Trubner, 1935), 7, and part 3: *The Logical Syntax of Language*, trans. Amethe Smeaton (London: Routledge & Kegan Paul, 1937), 279, 315, 331–32; "Philosophical Problems," in *The Philosophy of Rudolf Carnap*, ed. Paul Arthur Schilpp (La Salle: Open Court; London: Cambridge University Press, 1963), 44–86; in the same volume, see also Charles Morris's essay, 87–98, and Carnap's response, 860–62.

20. A. J. Ayer, *Language, Truth and Logic*, 48, 51, 57, 59, 152–53, esp. 59, 152–53.

21. Gilbert Ryle, "Systematically Misleading Expressions," in *Logic and Language*, 1st series, A. G. N. Flew ed. (Oxford: Basil Blackwell, 1951), 11, 36, esp. 36; cf. *The Concept of Mind* (London: Hutchinson's University Library, 1949), 7–8.

22. F. Waismann, *The Principles of Linguistic Philosophy*, ed. R. Harré (London: Macmillan; New York: St Martin's, 1965), 8–14.

23. A good many contemporary philosophers, unwilling, for reasons never explained, to abandon the designation "analytic philosophy" after they have clearly abandoned its defining metaphilosophical theses, have taken to designating philosophy in the classical world tradition too as "analytical philosophy." Thus David M. Armstrong writes: "Since that time [the time of the Vienna Circle, Wittgenstein, and Ryle], philosophers in the 'analytic tradition' have swung back from Wittgensteinian and Rylean pessimism to a more traditional conception of the proper role and tasks of philosophy.

Many analytic philosophers now would accept the view that the central task of philosophy is to give an account, or at least play a part in giving an account, of the general nature of things and man. (I would include myself among that many.)" *The Nature of Mind and Other Essays* (Ithaca: Cornell University Press, 1981), 17.

That is not my usage in the present essay. My usage—underlying which is a general principle of terminology—is that when the essential metaphilosophical doctrines of the analytic conception of philosophy have been abandoned in favor of the essential metaphilosophical doctrines of the classical world tradition, the designation too ought to be abandoned. That in reverse is in fact what the major early analytic philosophers—Carnap, Schlick, Ayer, and others—did when they jettisoned the metaphilosophical doctrines of the classical world tradition without being evasive about it, and rightly so.

For more recent examples of such misleading uses of "analytical philosophy," see Bernard Williams, *Ethics and the Limits of Philosophy* (Cambridge: Harvard University Press, 1985), vii–viii; D. W. Hamlyn, *A History of Western Philosophy* (New York: Viking Penguin, 1987; London: Penguin, 1988), chap. 17; and Thomas Nagel, *Mortal Questions* (Cambridge: Cambridge University Press, 1979), ix. Hao Wang's search for a clear and true conception of analytic philosophy is instructive but inconclusive. See his *Beyond Analytic Philosophy: Doing Justice to What We Know* (Cambridge: MIT Press, A Bradford Book, 1986), x–xi, 24 n. 23, 32, 100.

24. As in Wittgenstein, *Tractatus*, 6.42–6.421; in Carnap, *The Unity of Science*, 21–24, esp. 23–24, and *Philosophy and Logical Syntax*, 22–26, esp. 23; in Ayer, *Language, Truth and Logic*, chap. 6, esp. 102–12; and in Hans Reichenbach, *The Rise of Scientific Philosophy* (Berkeley: University of California Press, 1951), chap. 17, esp. 276–80.

25. As in A. J. Ayer, *Philosophical Essays* (London: Macmillan; New York: St. Martin's 1954), 245–49, esp. 245–46; in Arthur Pap, *Elements of Analytic Philosophy* (New York: Macmillan, 1949), 12–16, esp. 13, and chap. 2; in R. M. Hare, *The Language of Morals* (Oxford: Clarendon, 1952); in Stephen Toulmin, *An Examination of The Place of Reason in Ethics* (Cambridge: Cambridge University Press, 1950); and in Charles L. Stevenson, *Ethics and Language* (New Haven: Yale University Press, 1944).

26. As in Wittgenstein, *Tractatus*, 6.53; in Carnap, *The Unity of Science*, 22–23, and "The Elimination of Metaphysics Through Logical Analysis of Language" in *Philosophy and Logical Syntax*, part 1, 9–38, (reprinted in *Logical Positivism*, A. J. Ayer, ed. 60–81); in Ayer, *Language, Truth and Logic*, chap. 1; and C. G. Hempel, "The Empiricist Criterion of Meaning," reprinted in *Logical Positivism*, ed. Ayer, 108–132, esp. 108–9.

27. P. F. Strawson, *Individuals: A Descriptive Metaphysics* (London: Methuen, 1959), 9.

28. As in Carnap, *The Unity of Science*, 23, and *Philosophy and Logical Syntax*, 18–22; and in Richard Rorty, *Philosophy and the Mirror of Nature* (Princeton: Princeton University Press, 1979), introduction, esp. 7, and chaps. 3–4.

29. As in Wittgenstein, *Tractatus*, 4.1121 ("Theory of knowledge is the philosophy of psychology"); in Carnap, "The Elimination of Metaphysics Through Logical Analysis" (where theory of knowledge is equated with applied logic, which is explained as clarification of the cognitive content of scientific statements by means of logical analysis) reprinted in *Logical Positivism*, ed. Ayer, 60; in Carnap, *Philosophy and Logical Syntax*, 82–83; and in Hamlyn, *The Theory of Knowledge*, for which see section 2.3.

30. *The Philosophy of Bertrand Russell*, ed. Schilpp, 729.

31. T. D. Weldon, *The Vocabulary of Politics* (London: Penguin, 1953), chap. 1.

32. G. E. Moore, *Principia Ethica* (Cambridge: Cambridge University Press, 1903), vii, 26: and "A Defence of Common Sense," in *Philosophical Papers* (London: George Allen & Unwin; New York: Macmillan, 1959), esp. 32, 53, 58–59.

Enlarging upon these themes, F. Waismann writes: "Previous philosophers have almost always directed their attention to the *answers* given in reply to philosophical questions. . . .The great mistake of philosophers up to now, which has led to so many misunderstandings, is that they have produced answers before seeing clearly the nature of the questions they have been asking. They seem to have been quite unaware of the possibility that the form of the question itself might conceal an error" (*Principles*, 3–4). If that *was* a mistake of philosophers up to now, it was not a mistake made by Siddhattha Gotama, the Buddha; for, according to the Pali Canon, the Buddha was known by his contemporaries in the India of the sixth century B.C. as a *vibhajja-vādi*—an analytic teacher— and he divided all philosophical questions into four classes: questions to be answered categorically, definitely, or directly (*pañho ekaṁsavyākaraniyo*); questions to be "answered" with a counterquestion (*pañho patipuccha-vyākaraniyo*); questions to be set aside, or rejected, as wrongly formulated (*pañho-thāpaniyo*); and finally questions to be "answered" with a prior analysis of the question before being answered directly and categorically (*pañho vi bhajja-vyākaranīyo*). In the Canon, this classification of philosophical questions is to be found in *Aṅguttara Nikāya*, ed. R. Morris and E. Hardy, 5 vols. (London: Pali Text Society, 1885–1900), i.196; in English translation in F. L. Woodward, *The Book of the Gradual Sayings* (London: Pali Text Society, 1932), 1:178–79; and explained and illustrated at length in K. N. Jayatilleke, *Early Buddhist Theory of Knowledge* (London: George Allen & Unwin, 1963), 281–93.

33. Hamlyn, *Theory of Knowledge*, 9.

34. Wittgenstein, *Philosophical Investigations*, 109, 128.

35. Ryle, *Concept of Mind*, 7–9.

36. Strawson, *Individuals*, 10.

37. Ayer, *Language, Truth and Logic*, chap. 6; *Philosophical Essay*, 245–49; *Philosophy in the Twentieth Century*, 15–16.

38. Anthony Kenny, *Wittgenstein* (Middlesex: Penguin-Pelican, 1973–76), 203.

39. Arthur C. Danto, *What Philosophy Is: A Guide to the Elements* (New York: Harper & Row, 1968), 145–46; cf. his *Analytical Philosophy of Knowledge* (Cambridge: Cambridge University Press, 1968). Danto still subscribes to very much the same outlook; see his *Connections to the World*.

40. For Hamlyn's treatment of general skepticism, see *Theory of Knowledge*, part 1 (and chap. 10 in part 3); for his treatment of limited skepticism, part 2 (and, again, chap. 10 in part 3). For Ayer's treatment of limited skepticisms, see *The Problem of Knowledge*, chaps. 2–5. For Pollock's treatment of general skepticism, see *Knowledge and Justification*, 6–11; for his treatment of limited skepticisms, chaps. 3, 7, 8, 9, 10.

In both his book, *The History of Scepticism from Erasmus to Spinoza*, rev. ed. (Berkeley: University of California Press, 1979), and an article, "Skepticism," *Encyclopedia of Philosophy* 7:449–61, Richard H. Popkin uses the term "extreme" for a conception approximating Hamlyn's "general" and the terms "limited" and "mitigated" for a conception approximating Hamlyn's limited forms.

41. Such accounts may be contrasted with that of Chisholm, "The Theory of Knowledge," in *Philosophy*, ed. P. Schlatter (Englewood Cliffs, N.J.: Prentice-Hall, 1965), chap. 1, 244–52, where he discusses all the forms of skepticism ignored by the writers cited. The essay is reprinted as part 3 of his *The Foundations of Knowing* (Sussex: Harvester, 1982).

Although Pollock mentions the possibility of moral skepticism, the problem is never again raised in his book and he makes no attempt to counter it as he does all the others.

42. For Danto, see *What Philosophy Is*, 9–11, 145–48; for Ayer, see *The Problem of Knowledge*, chap. 1. Danto's position in *Connections to the World* is only a refinement of his earlier position, which remains essentially the same.

43. David Hume, *A Treatise of Human Nature* (Oxford: Clarendon, 1888), 1.4.1.

44. Norman Kemp Smith, *The Philosophy of David Hume* (New York: St Martin's, 1941), 325; cf. 361–62, 546. See also Donald M. Frame, trans., *The Complete Essays of Montaigne* (Stanford: Stanford University Press, 1965, 370–419 (on skepticism generally), esp. 371–76 (on Pyrrho and Pyrrhonism); and Pierre Bayle, "Pyrrho," in *The Dictionary Historical and Critical*, 2d ed. (London: 1734–38). I owe thanks to Roderick Chisholm for this reference to Bayle's *Dictionary*. It was he who drew my attention to it, without, however, indicating what I would find in it or why he thought I should look into it.

Thomas Reid, Hume's contemporary and a severe critic of what he took to be the skepticisms of Hume and Berkeley, never, to the best of my knowledge, formulated a general conception of skepticism; but he did think the skepticisms of Hume and Berkeley were traceable to "Pyrrho the Elean, the father of this philosophy"—in Reid's own words, "giving no credit to the senses"; *The Works of Thomas Reid*, ed. Sir William Hamilton, 4th ed. (London: Longmans, Green, 1854), 167. But the only source he cites for this judgment is "Antigonus the Carystian, quoted by Diogenes Laertius." There is no evidence that he based his judgment on the Pyrrho-text, or even knew of its existence; and there is no evidence of the Pyrrho-text in Diogenes Laertius.

45. As in A. J. Ayer, *Philosophical Essays*, 170.
46. Myles Burnyeat, ed., *The Skeptical Tradition* (Berkeley: University of California Press, 1983), 1.
47. The reader will search the works of the philosophers just cited in vain for such citations: Wittgenstein's *Tractatus, Philosophical Investigations*, and *On Certainty;* Quine's numerous books and papers (e.g., the paper already cited), most recently *The Philosophy of W. V. Quine* (1986), in the Library of Living Philosophers; Ryle's *Dilemmas*, chap. 7 of which is wholly devoted to skepticism with respect to sense perception; Ayer's *Philosophical Essays, The Problem of Knowledge, The Concept of a Person and Other Essays*, and *The Central Questions of Philosophy;* and the two works of Arthur Danto already cited. Danto's latest work is no different; see *Connections to the World*, 200–202. The more things change, the more they remain the same.
48. W. V. Quine, "Mr. Strawson on Logical Theory," *Mind*, 42, no. 248 (October 1953):433–51; the passage quoted is on p. 449. Reprinted in Quine, *The Ways of Paradox and Other Essays* (New York: Random, 1966), 152.
49. Chisholm, "Theory of Knowledge," in *Philosophy*, 242.
50. Hamlyn, "Epistemology"; *Sensation and Perception: A History of the Philosophy of Perception* (London: Routledge & Kegan Paul, 1961); "Greek Philosophy after Aristotle," in *A Critical History of Western Philosophy*, ed. D. J. O'Connor (New York: Free Press, 1964), chap. 4; and *Theory of Knowledge*.
In *Scepticism: A Critical Reappraisal* (Oxford: Basil Blackwell, 1980), Nicholas Rescher, like Hamlyn, takes care to document the skeptical adversary, but that adversary does not consist of philosophical skeptics of all significant sorts but only the sort who repudiate the possibility of factual knowledge.
51. *Theory of Knowledge*, 7, 22; "Epistemology", 9.
In the most massive philosophical and scholarly study of the pre-Socratic philosophers ever written (to the best of my knowledge), Jonathan Barnes writes, "The sceptical philosophers of Hellenistic Greece held that no one at all could know anything at all; and with commendable consistency they proceeded to deny that they themselves knew that distressing fact"; *The Presocratic Philosophers*, rev. ed. (London: Routledge & Kegan Paul, 1982), 136. He cites half a dozen ancient Greek skeptics not cited by Hamlyn and not belonging to the schools Hamlyn cites, all of whom I deal with in section 2.1.

2. Examination of Some Theses of the New Epistemology

1. See note 5.
2. In Barnes, *The Presocratic Philosophers*, 559–60 (Democritus), 559 and 562 (Metrodorus of Chios), 562 (Leucippus), and 137–38 (Xenophanes).
3. My principal source for Sextus Empiricus is R. G. Bury, trans., *Sextus Empiricus*, 4 vols., Loeb Classical Library (Cambridge: Harvard University Press, 1933). References to this work are hereafter cited in the text. Instead of adopting the esoteric system of abbreviations and references customary among classical scholars, I adopt the much simpler and clearer one used by Bury: "I" for his introduction in volume 1 to the four volumes of his translation; "P" for *Outlines of Pyrrhonism;* "L" for *Against the Logicians;* "Ph" for *Against the Physicists;* and "E" for *Against the Ethicists*. I supplement all that with "Pr" for *Against the Professors* (the *Mathematici*), an abbreviation which for some reason Bury did not provide.
The four volumes of this edition contain the full Greek text on the facting page. In the present work, the translations of passages in *Outlines of Pyrrhonism* and *Against the professors* (the *Mathematici*) are Bury's, except where otherwise noted—the exceptions occurring mainly with respect to those texts widely construed as expressions of general skepticism. See note 16 and section 2.1.3.
4. Bury, *Sextus Empiricus* 3:515; Hamlyn, "Greek Philosophy after Aristotle," 73; John Burnet, "Sceptics," in *Encyclopaedia of Religion and Ethics*, ed. J. Hastings, 12 vols. (Edinburgh, 1908–26), 11:229.
5. All or some of my eleven theses are denied by major twentieth-century students of Greek Skepticism: e.g., Bury, *Sextus Empiricus* 1: vii, xxix, and 3:515; Charlotte L. Stough, *Greek Skepticism: A Study in Epistemology* (Berkeley: University of California Press, 1969), 4, 146; Barnes,

The Presocratic Philosophers, 136–37; Julia Annas and Jonathan Barnes, *The Modes of Scepticism; Ancient Texts and Modern Interpretations* (Cambridge: Cambridge University Press, 1985), 8, 17, 23, 45, and throughout; Myles Burnyeat, "Can the Skeptic Live His Skepticism?" in *The Skeptical Tradition,* 119, 127; Rescher, *Scepticism,* 10–15; Popkin, "Skepticism," 449–61, esp. 450, and *The History of Scepticism from Erasmus to Spinoza,* xiii–xxi, esp. xiii–xv; and A. A. Long and D. N. Sedley, *The Hellenistic Philosophers,* 2 vols. (vol. 1, *Translations of the Principal Sources, with Philosophical Commentary;* vol. 2, *Greek and Latin Texts with Notes and Bibliography* [Cambridge: Cambridge University Press, 1987]), 1:473–88. Annas and Barnes, e.g., cite the text (P.i.9) which I have cited, taking it at face value; see their *Modes,* 25.

Hegel is an eighteenth/nineteenth-century student who denies some of these theses; see note 17. Chisholm is one twentieth-century student who recognizes that Sextus Empiricus was not a general skeptic; see his "Sextus Empiricus and Modern Empiricism," *Philosophy of Science* 8 (July, 1941), part 2, esp. 376–78.

It has been brought to my attention by Richard Watson and Charles Young that in a recent work, *Essays in Ancient Philosophy* (Minneapolis: University of Minnesota Press, 1987), Michael Frede has defended a view about Pyrrhonian skepticism which is similar to mine, and they ask me to sort out the points of similarity and difference—I shall henceforth speak in addition of agreements and disagreements—between our two treatments. Frede's relevant essays are "The Skeptic's Beliefs" (which appeared first in German in 1979 and in English translation in *Essays*) and "The Skeptic's Two Kinds of Assent and the Possibility of Knowledge" (in English, 1984). My attention has been directed especially to the following passage:

> According to [the usual interpretation of Pyrrhonian skepticism], the skeptic not only claims to have no deeper insight into things, he also claims not to know anything at all. . . . The skeptic refuses to assent to any proposition.
>
> Any interpretation along these lines, however, seems fundamentally mistaken to me. No matter how ingenious he may be, the skeptic cannot avoid knowing many things. (*Essays,* 179)

There are indeed many points of similarity and difference, of agreement and disagreement, between our two treatments—so many that I cannot possibly deal with them adequately or even fairly in this note. I shall, however, indicate some of the similarities and differences and some of the agreements and disagreements as summarily as possible.

We agree that, according to Sextus Empiricus, "the skeptic, in many instances, does think of himself as knowing something" (*Essays,* 180). I indicate that there are thousands of such instances.

We agree that such claims to knowledge are "perfectly compatible with his skepticism" (*Essays,* 180).

We agree that on what Frede calls "the usual interpretation of Pyrrhonian skepticism" (although he does not identify those interpreters), "the skeptical position turns out to be inconsistent" (*Essays,* 180).

We agree that the (Pyrrhonian) skeptic can have and does have beliefs (*Essays,* 180, 189, 192).

We agree on the dubious value of Timon's testimony concerning Pyrrho's views (*Essays,* 182–83).

We cite a substantial number of the same skeptical texts—especially those of Sextus Empiricus—in support of the same interpretations of skepticism.

The list of similarities and agreements could go on; but the list of differences and disagreements is, it seems to me, even greater and more striking. Among those numerous differences and disagreements are the following:

He holds that there are no views or beliefs that define Pyrrhonian skepticism (*Essays,* 179). I think there are and have indicated what some of them are, doing little more in fact than report the explicit statements and definitions of Sextus Empiricus himself.

He holds that there are no specific doctrines or dogmas which a Skeptic, rather than a member of one of the Dogmatic schools, would have. That judgment, it seems to me, is true for dogmas (as defined by Sextus) but false for doctrines, many of which I have specified.

He holds that Pyrrhonian skepticism is not "characterized by specifically skeptical views that rely on 'deeper' insights into the true nature of things" (*Essays*, 179), while I hold that one of the specifically "skeptical" views (in Sextus's sense) does rely on a deeper insight into the true nature of things when those things are philosophical *theories*, for one kind of example. According to Sextus, the Dogmatists and the Academics are both mistaken, the Dogmatists thinking that they have discovered philosophical truth, and the Academics thinking that philosophical truth is undiscoverable.

He holds that "even the phrase, 'nothing is to be known,' is not accepted by the skeptical philosopher as expressing a skeptical doctrine (Sext. Emp. P.H. I 200)" (*Essays*, 129); I argue (in section 2.1.2.2) that it is, at least by Sextus Empiricus himself, once he has reformulated it. And then too, at this point, "the peculiar feature of classical Greek" comes into play. I would just add, without comment, that the Greek for which Frede gives "nothing is to be known" is *panta estin akatalēpta*, which does not seem to me to be correctly translatable as "all is unknown" *or* "all is unknowable." Philosophically, the point is important; and the word *katalēptos* is another of those verbal adjectives from which those alpha-privatives are derived, in this case *akatalēpta*.

The differences between our treatments are also numerous and striking.

Perhaps the biggest and most significant difference is in our respective overall outlooks. In the two essays cited, his approach seems to be mainly that of a classical scholar trying to determine the truth about "the skeptic," mainly "the Pyrrhonian skeptic." Mine is mainly philosophical: I am trying essentially to determine the truth about the nature of epistemology and the nature of philosophy in opposition to the most influential school of philosophy in the twentieth century, that of analytic philosophy. My concern with philosophical skepticism, whether general or restricted, is mainly rooted in the alleged connections (definitional, chronological or historical, and genetic, etc.) between general skepticism, epistemology, and philosophy (including its two additional branches—metaphysics and moral philosophy). I do not think that *any* branch of philosophy is essentially prompted by general philosophical skepticism; and I think that philosophy in the twentieth century has gone badly astray in its preoccupation with general skepticism.

Another is that my central focus in the present work is on the concept of knowledge; my references to belief, assent, speech or assertion, judgment, argument, proposition and doubt, and so forth are secondary. His focus seems to be just the reverse: in the two essays cited, the skeptic's claim to knowledge is set aside; it is the possibility of skeptical belief that forms his main concern in the first essay (*Essays*, 180), and skeptical assent that forms the main concern of his second.

A third is that in those essays at least, his focus is upon Sextus Empiricus; Pyrrho is mentioned in passing and then put aside. My focus in section 2.1 is equally upon both, devoting a great deal of critical attention to the Pyrrho-text, which he neither deals with nor mentions.

A fourth is that in addition to Sextus and Pyrrho I deal with the remaining Greek Skeptics, the major Greek Sophists, and "the odds and ends"—for example, Metrodorus of Chios; he does not.

A fifth is that in the course of dealing with Sextus and Pyrrho I elicit four principles of interpretation with the help of which I deal with all those other ancient skeptics.

A sixth is my focus on what I call "a strange feature of classical Greek," which looms large in my argument; in his essays there is no mention of that feature—possibly because he does not think it *is* a feature of classical Greek, or that even if it is a feature it is unimportant. I have noted in my text that I have been unable to find any discussion or even any reference in the scholarly classical literature to this peculiar feature.

6. It is curious that G. E. Moore's general account of what philosophy is—an account which he never repudiated, evidence that he was never one of those who subscribe to an analytic conception of philosophy—is traceable to Sextus Empiricus, whose account is traceable to the early Stoics; G. E. Moore, *Some Main Problems of Philosophy* (London: Allen & Unwin; New York: Macmillan, 1953), chap. 1.

7. Cf. Chisholm's judgment that "epistemologists presuppose . . . that they can succeed. This means, therefore, that they have a kind of faith in themselves"; *Theory of Knowledge*, 3d ed., 5.

8. All this, and the rest of section 2.1, makes clear the extreme inadequacy of Quine's conception of skepticism, and consequently the inadequacy of his critical response to skepticism.

9. In *The Modes of Skepticism* Annas and Barnes write: "There are passages in Sextus' work in which he poses as a defender of Common Sense and an opponent only of scientific and philosophical dogmatism . . . By and large the Ten Modes are designed to produce a radical skepticism" (124). My view is that he was not posing and that the Ten Tropes are not designed to produce a "radical"

(i.e., utterly general) skepticism. The evidence Annas and Barnes cite in support of their interpretation is highly incomplete; see note 13.

10. E.g., Rescher, *Scepticism,* chap. 1, esp. 10–11. The passage from Montaigne's *Apology for Raymond Sebond* which Rescher quotes at that point shows how Montaigne misinterpreted the Greek Skeptics, and how as a consequence Hume was misled in turn, depending as he did upon secondary sources and worse. See note 44 to chapter 1.

Of all the world's epistemologists known to me, the one who has most strenuously grappled with "the problem of the criterion" is R. M. Chisholm; see, e.g., his *Theory of Knowledge,* 2d ed. (Englewood Cliffs, N.J.: Prentice-Hall, 1977), chap. 7; *The Foundations of Knowing,* chap. 5; *Theory of Knowledge,* 3d ed., (1989), 6–7, 36.

11. In *The Modes of Skepticism,* 22, 124, Annas and Barnes argue that Sextus Empiricus *is* a general skeptic; but their translations and discussions of his account of the Ten Tropes are very incomplete, omitting much of the most important evidential data that I cite. Long and Sedley do the same; cf. *The Hellenistic Philosophers* 1:473.

12. In *Modes* (17, 166–68), Annas and Barnes do just that; but so does Montaigne (*Complete Essays,* 372), although nothing could be clearer than Sextus' explanation of the double dimension of the Skeptic's End.

13. Where the content of Skeptic doctrine is concerned, Bury's lengthy introduction to the Loeb edition consists wholly of interpretations, apparently assuming them to be so evident that substantiating evidence does not need to be cited (although interpretations in his numerous footnotes to his translation are tied to particular passages and terms). Annas and Barnes (*Modes*) cite evidence drawn mainly from the first group; Stough (*Greek Skepticism*), in her chapter on Sextus, cites evidence drawn mainly from the third; and Hamlyn cites no evidence. I know of no student of Greek Skepticism who takes account of all the evidence marshaled in these pages, or even much of it.

14. E.g., Annas and Barnes, *Modes,* 2, 8, 9, 25.

15. E.g., by Stough, *Greek Skepticism,* 26–28; by Annas and Barnes, *Modes,* 11, 25; by Rescher, *Scepticism,* 15, 5; and by Montaigne, *Complete Essays,* 373–74.

16. These possible variations in the translation of the Greek will be discussed in section 2.1.3, especially in the section on Pyrrho, and their significance assessed.

17. Stough, *Greek Skepticism,* 141, 146. In Hegel's *Introduction to the Lectures on the History of Philosophy,* trans. T. M. Knox and A. V. Miller (Oxford: Oxford University Press, 1985; Clarendon Press, 1987), 181, Hegel writes: "Among the Greeks, we have to consider the philosophy of sophists and skeptics. They have propounded the doctrine that the truth *cannot* be known" (emphasis added).

My references here and in note 5 to Hegel have prompted one of the editors, Richard A. Watson, to suggest that I add something about Michael N. Forster's *Hegel and Skepticism* (Cambridge: Harvard University Press, 1989), which has just been published and so has been unavailable to me for present purposes (except in a photocopy of its introduction, first two chapters, and associated notes, provided by Watson). In these comments I shall on the whole confine myself to those views of Hegel (and Forster) which bear on what I have previously said, leaving consideration of the much larger questions raised by Forster's valuable and welcome study to another venue.

In note 5 I say, in the context of the eleven theses which I advance about Sextus Empiricus, that "Hegel is an eighteenth/nineteenth-century student [of philosophical skepticism] who denies some" of those eleven theses. Among his theses which I deny (since his statement of his views antedates mine by two centuries) are the following:

1. that Sextus—and more generally "radical ancient skepticism, and particularly Pyrrhonism as preserved in the writings of Sextus Empiricus" (*Hegel,* 9)—is a general skeptic;
2. that the suspense-of-judgment (*epochē*) for which Sextus and the Pyrrhonists argue is general or universal (*Hegel,* 9);
3. that "the older (i.e., Pyrrhonian) skepticism . . . proves the untruth of all" (*Hegel,* 36); and
4. that the principle and method of equipollence (*isostheneia:* equal logical force) is absolutely general in scope (*Hegel,* 10).

Against Hegel's thesis 1 the whole of section 2.2.2 is a sustained argument. Against his thesis 2 is my seventh thesis, for which I argue on pages 16–18. Against his thesis 3 are my antitheses stated in the form of the third, the fourth, the fifth, and the sixth theses (p. 13), some of the arguments for which are presented on pages 14–16, then headon in page 21, and earlier by way of preparatory considerations on pages 19–21 (the elliptical character of many of Sextus' crucial "skeptical" formulations). Against Hegel's thesis 4 I argue on page 19. Neither in Hegel (according to Forster) nor in Forster (when he is stating his own views) is there any reference to Sextus' explanations of the elliptical character of many of his skeptical formulations, and the limited scope of those formulations when the ellipticity is eliminated.

Sometimes when Forster takes issue with one of Hegel's interpretations, he seems to me to advance misinterpretations of his own. Thus with respect to thesis 3, above, Forster says that "the ancient skeptics did not aim to prove anything and did not attempt to show in any way that claims were untrue" (*Hegel*, 36). But in fact they—at any rate Sextus—did: e.g., at L.ii.17–18 (one of numerous similar passages in his work), where in the space of two sentences (about truth itself) he says "as we shall prove," "as we shall demonstrate," and "as we shall establish." Whether in saying these things Sextus was contradicting his general philosophical outlook is another question, irrelevant to the question whether he ever aimed to prove anything.

Throughout the present work I have protested against the use of expressions like "the ancient skeptics" in the context of assertions like many of those of Hegel and Forster. Following Burnyeat, I have pointed out that much of the writing on skepticism by Hume, Montaigne, Wittgenstein, Ayer, Quine, Ryle, "and numerous others" is conducted in a kind of philosophical vacuum into which Quine himself falls after having himself protested against it ("Strawson v. Strawman"). Given, for example, that all that survives of the writings of Metrodorus of Chios—*one* of those "ancient skeptics"—is a single sentence (p. 28; see pp. 35–6 for a typical interpretation of it by Jonathan Barnes), we are in no position to say what he aimed to prove or whether or not he aimed to prove anything at all. As for Pyrrho—another of "the ancient skeptics"—what we have in terms of the Pyrrho-text certainly provides reason to believe that he was trying to prove something: sentence 3 in that text is advanced as a reason for believing sentence 4; and the unnumbered sentence following 4 starts with "therefore." As for Sextus, he argues at great length that *all* the centuries-old disagreements and controversies about matters philosophical, scientific, and artistic (*philosophia, epistemē, kai technē*) are, if not absolutely unresolvable, at any rate unresolved, and that suspense-of-judgment with respect to all of them is for the time being and under the circumstances the wisest course to take and the only course leading to *ataraxia* and *eudaimonia*. On page 17 I cite numerous logical and other principles and techniques to which he appeals, and the passages in which he appeals to them, all of which look to me like "attempts to prove something."

Earlier in this note I quoted Hegel's judgment that the Greek Sophists and Skeptics "have propounded the doctrine that the truth cannot be known." This judgment is weaker than his judgment, earlier quoted, that "the older skepticism . . . proves the untruth of all."

First concerning the Greek Skeptics: Sextus I have already dealt with in this note. As for Pyrrho and Pyrrhonism, I argue at length in section 2.2.3 not that there is (as I think there is in the case of Sextus) conclusive or all but conclusive reason to believe that he is not a general skeptic, but that there is "woefully insufficient reason" to believe that he is. The argument in his case is rather intricate and involves (1) translations and interpretations of a number of crucial terms in the Pyrrho-text; (2) "a more fundamental question," the absence of certain epistemic terms from the Pyrrho-text which one would expect to find if Pyrrho were opting for general skepticism; (3) the "still more fundamental question," that is, that general skepticism in any philosophically significant sense must be formulated in modal, not nonmodal, terms; (4) the even more fundamental fact which I characterize as "the strange feature of classical Greek" concerning its use of verbal adjectives, especially the negative ones called alpha-privatives; (5) the significance of that feature when combined with the extraordinary brevity of the Pyrrho-text; and finally (6), the four principles of interpretation, which, I argue, must be satisfied "if an isolated philosophical text (e.g., that of Metrodorus of Chios or of Pyrrho-Timon) is to be adequately interpreted and even translated," and which, I argue, is not satisfied by the Pyrrho-Timon text. Neither Hegel (according to Forster) nor Forster (in his own voice) takes account of any of these six considerations in his critical examination and interpretation of "the ancient skeptics." But, to the best of my knowledge, neither does any other student of ancient philosophical skepticism. I would on that account tend to think that something must be wrong with my account; but given these considerations, I see no way to avoid my conclusion. Perhaps Forster can.

As for the remaining Greek Skeptics, although I have made as exhaustive a study of all of them (Timon of Phlius, Arcesilaus of Pitane, Carneades of Cyrene, Aenesidemus, Agrippa, and others) as I have of Sextus, with the same result (that there is insufficient reason to interpret them as general skeptics), nevertheless when I hit upon the four principles of interpretation and saw (or thought I saw) that the latter could be used to circumvent all the scholarship, the amassing of the evidence, and the tripling of the size of the study, that is what I did; I then extended the maneuver to take in the Greek Sophists (for whom I have done what I have done for all the Greek Skeptics). The reader (especially the skeptical reader) is then free to do either of two things: carry out the application on his own, concluding either that I am right about my prediction or that I am wrong; or insist that I carry it out on my own in public. A third alternative is to judge the project wrongheaded to begin with and so not worth carrying out.

Very much to my surprise, given that I received my philosophical education or miseducation in schools heavily influenced or dominated by analytic philosophy (whose classical literature portrays Hegel in the most repulsive terms), I find myself agreeing with or sympathetic to much of Hegel's outlook on philosophical skepticism—for example, his judgment that ancient skepticism is philosophically superior to (what in his day counted as) modern skepticism (*Hegel,* chap. 1). The presentation of philosophical skepticism in Sextus Empiricus seems to me incomparably superior to anything to be found in modern philosophy in point of scope, depth, system, and exhaustiveness. Neither Wittgenstein nor Quine—to single out two twentieth-century writers most highly regarded by the generality of their colleagues—has even begun to come to grips with that system. I have already mentioned Chisholm as one of the rare contemporary philosophers who has.

Despite my criticism of Hegel (and in passing of Forster), I should like to conclude by saying that I am thankful to Forster for bringing this widely overlooked dimension of Hegel's general philosophy to the philosophical community's attention (and I am therefore thankful to Watson for bringing Forster's study to my attention). As Forster writes, "Hegel's reflections on the nature of the skeptical tradition have considerable intrinsic merit, containing original insights from which contemporary historians of philosophy and philosophers concerned with skepticism can profit" (*Hegel,* 1). In the familiar works on Hegel—Stace, Mure, and Findlay—there is no hint of any of this; nor is there any hint of it in D. W. Hamlyn's "History of Epistemology" or in Richard Popkin's historical survey, "Skepticism" (*Encyclopedia of Philosophy,* Edwards, 7:449–61), covering the period from the fifth century B.C. to the twentieth century A.D., or in his *The High Road to Pyrrhonism* ("selected studies in eighteenth-century philosophy, with one excursion into the nineteenth").

Hamlyn, *A History of Western Philosophy,* 35, 83, 85–87, repeats Hegel's judgment of the skeptics, and so the error survives century after century.

18. Bury, *Sextus Empiricus* 1:vii, xxix–xxxvi; Hamlyn, *Theory of Knowledge,* 8, but especially "Greek Philosophy after Aristotle," in *A Critical History of Western Philosophy,* chap. 4, 72–73, and most recently in *A History of Western Philosophy,* 77, 83, 85, 86, esp. 83; Stough, *Greek Skepticism,* 4, 16–34, 146; A. A. Long, *Hellenistic Philosophy,* 2d ed. (Berkeley: University of California Press, 1986), 79–82; D. N. Sedley, "The Motivation of Greek Skepticism," 9–29, esp. 14–15; Barnes, *The Presocratic Philosophers,* 136–37; Annas and Barnes, *Modes,* 10–12; and Long and Sedley, *The Hellenistic Philosophers* 1:13–24, esp. 14–18. Russell's account of Pyrrho, in *A History of Western Philosophy,* 233–35, is appallingly inaccurate; he appears not to have read even the secondary or tertiary sources with any care.

All these works are Western; but a recent Eastern or non-Western account of philosophical skepticism advances many of the interpretations of Pyrrho and the later Pyrrhonists with which I take issue; see A. S. Bogomolov, *History of Ancient Philosophy: Greece and Rome* (Moscow: Progress, 1985), 305–18.

19. The handful of facts just summarized are known to all the specialists in Greek Skepticism, but nowhere in the works of any of those specialists are those facts collected in one place and set out clearly so as to make clear their collective significance, which is important.

20. In every work in the Library of Living Philosophers in which the philosopher subjected to critical scrutiny responds, the philosopher laments the misunderstandings of his writings.

21. Long and Sedley, *The Hellenistic Philosophers* 2:5; F Aristocles (Eusebius, *Pr. ev.* 14.18.1–5; Caizzi 53).

22. Long and Sedley, *The Hellenistic Philosophers* 1:14–15.

23. Burnet, "Sceptics," 229.

24. Stough, *Greek Skepticism,* 17; hereafter cited in text.

25. Long, *Hellenistic Philosophy,* 80–81.

26. Sedley, "The Motivation of Greek Skepticism," 24, 14.

27. Annas and Barnes, *Modes,* 11.

28. On this point, see Burnet, *Early Greek Philosophy,* the introduction (1–30, but esp. 10–11) and the appendix ("On the meaning of φύσις"), 363–64; and Guthrie, *A History of Greek Philosophy* 1:55, 73, 82, 83, esp. 82, 83.

29. Sedley's predicate—"undifferentiated"—seems no less unwarranted than his subject, "The world." Among the five senses of *adiaphora* listed in the unabridged *Greek-English Lexicon* of Liddell and Scott, the nearest to Sedley's "undifferentiated" is "having no logical differentia," which is presumably the source—Sedley himself does not explain—of Sedley's "undifferentiated." But the *Lexicon* itself seems to be in error: the text—Aristotle's *Metaphysics* 1016ª18—it cites in justification of its listing of "having no logical differentia" in fact says nothing to warrant the listing. That sense, therefore, should, it seems, be struck out of the *Lexicon;* and, if so, then Sedley's "undifferentiated" too has no warrant. In *The Hellenistic Philosophers* (1:16–17), Sedley and Long set forth their joint interpretation of the Pyrrho-text, which they later characterize as "the metaphysical interpretation . . . instead of the narrowly epistemological reading fashionable since Zeller" (2:6).

30. Sedley is one who does so; see *The Skeptical Tradition,* 14. The Greek original can be found in *Diogenes Laertius,* trans. R. D. Hicks, Loeb Classical Library (Cambridge: Harvard University Press, 1925), 2:478.

31. Sedley, "The Motivation of Greek Scepticism," 14.

32. There is a very good study of the possible links between Pyrrho and India by E. Flintoff, "Pyrrho and India," *Phronesis* 25 (1980): 88–108. To the best of my knowledge, that study has remained almost completely disregarded by Western students of Greek Skepticism. See, e.g., Annas and Barnes, *Modes,* 12, 193; Sedley, "The Motivation of Greek Scepticism," 15. Flintoff has not said all there is to be said about this matter, but his study constitutes a solid foundation for further scholarly exploration and philosophical theory.

33. It is a formulation accepted by many other students of philosophical skepticism—e.g., G. E. Moore, "Four Forms of Skepticism," in *Philosophical Papers,* 196–226, esp. 196; D. J. O'Connor and Brian Carr, *Introduction to the Theory of Knowledge* (Minneapolis: University of Minnesota Press, 1982), 2–3; Frede, *Essays,* 179, 201; Stough, *Greek Skepticism,* 4; and Annas and Barnes, *Modes,* 7, 12, 13.

34. Unable on my own to find verification of this feature in scholarly works accessible to me, I have consulted three classical scholars: Maria Asimakopolous, Jesuit High School, Carmichael, California; David Traill, Chair, Department of Classics, University of California at Davis; and Leslie Threatte, Department of Classics, University of California at Berkeley. The first said she was unaware of the feature; the second and third verified it immediately, but were unable to refer me to any works in which the feature was even mentioned, much less discussed and its implications drawn out. I owe thanks to all three for their generous responses to my numerous questions, but especially to Traill and Threatte.

Neither Burnet nor Guthrie nor any of the contributors to *The Pre-Socratics: A Collection of Critical Essays,* ed. Alexander P. D. Mourelatos (Garden City: Doubleday Anchor, 1974), nor G. S. Kirk and J. E. Raven, *The Presocratic Philosophers,* nor G. S. Kirk and J. E. Raven and M. Schofield, *The Pre-Socratic Philosophers,* nor Jonathan Barnes, *The Presocratic Philosophers,* mention the feature. In *Early Greek Philosophy* (Middlesex: Penguin, 1987),Jonathan Barnes devotes a major part of his introduction—sections 3, "The Evidence" and 4, "The Texts" (24–35)—to a discussion of problems of translation, and with all the essentials of that judicious and illuminating discussion I am in full agreement; but the feature of classical Greek to which I am drawing attention remains unmentioned in that discussion.

35. I have been unable to find any hint of such principles in any of the works accessible to me, e.g., those few mentioned in the preceding note.

36. Barnes, *The Presocratic Philosophers* (559), where he says that Metrodorus "purveys an extreme skepticism which foreshadows, in its ingenious comprehensiveness, the most extravagant claims of Pyrrho." He then goes on revealingly to admit that "of Metrodorus' book little else [but

that one sentence] survives and nothing to tell us what his scepticism rested upon." In *The Hellenistic Philosophers* (1:472), Long and Sedley espouse the same interpretation on the basis of the same sentence.

37. In section 1.4 I noted that Hamlyn cites the Greek Sophists, "especially . . . Gorgias . . . and Protagoras" (*Theory of Knowledge,* 8n.1), as major examples of general skeptics. It is therefore worth noting in the present context that in *The Sophistic Movement* (Cambridge: Cambridge University Press, 1981), 93–99, G. B. Kerferd critically discusses three conflicting interpretations of Gorgias' notorious "On That Which is Not, or on Nature"—conflicting interpretations still unresolved—and that in *The Presocratic Philosophers* Jonathan Barnes, unable to make any sense of that treatise, merely translates it (173–74, 182, 471) without comment—although in his 700-page tome he comments at length on every other text he deals with.

38. Barnes, *The Presocratic Philosophers,* 136, 144, 151.

39. Guthrie, for example, cites and discusses the epistemological speculations of Empedocles (*A History of Green Philosophy* 2:228–43), Anaxagoras (2:319–20), and Xenophanes (1:395–401)—in the case of Xenophanes even providing the heading "Theory of Knowledge" for the section on Xenophanes' epistemological speculations and adding that "the Sceptics of the fourth century B.C. and later seized eagerly on these lines as anticipation of their view that knowledge was unattainable." In fact, Guthrie provides the same heading, "Theory of Knowledge," for his discussion of Anaxagoras.

40. I have gathered a mass of evidence concerning the pre-Socratics to this effect and can cite it on demand, but do not do so in the present study out of considerations of brevity.

41. In *A History of Greek Philosophy,* Guthrie discusses the whole problem (4:41–54) and sets forth the conclusions which I have here adopted.

42. R. M. Chisholm, *Theory of Knowledge* (2d ed., 1977), 3, 120; also in "Theory of Knowledge," in *Philosophy,* 244; reprinted as "Theory of Knowledge in America," in *The Foundations of Knowing,* 113. In *Theory of Knowledge* (3d ed., 1989), 1, Chisholm reformulates these two traditional questions, but their gist remains the same.

43. Hamlyn, *Theory of Knowledge,* chap. 10, esp. secs. a and b. Hereafter cited in text.

44. That Hamlyn still subscribes to this conception of knowledge in the context of this conception of epistemology is clear from two recent works: *Metaphysics* (Cambridge: Cambridge University Press, 1984), vii; and *A History of Western Philosophy* (1988), which on its critical side repeats much (although sometimes with variations) of what we have already recorded of his views.

45. What I call "the classical conception or theory of epistemology" has been formulated but not so designated by Ernest Nagel in Ernest Nagel and Richard B. Brandt, eds., *Meaning and Knowledge: Systematic Readings in Epistemology* (New York: Harcourt, Brace & World, 1965), xi–xiii; Nagel characterizes it as "a fully adequate epistemology" instead of as "a complete epistemology." I adopt the latter designation partly because Hamlyn does and partly because of the notion of completeness in elementary logic, e.g., the notion of a complete logic of truth-functions and of general quantification, etc., which is relevant to my critical assessment of Hamlyn's notion. My account of it varies in some respects from Nagel's. Although Nagel does not say so, it seems to me that his conception of epistemology was formulated in large measure to fit the various aspects of Chisholm's epistemology.

46. See, e.g., W. V. Quine, *Philosophy of Logic* (Cambridge: Harvard University Press, 1970; 3d ed. 1986), chap. 5; W. V. Quine, *Methods of Logic* (New York: Holt, Rinehart and Winston, 1950; 3d ed. 1972), 73–76 (for truth-functions), 174ff., 182–83 (for quantification theory), and 226 (for identity theory).

47. Cf. Locke's account of his own purpose in his *An Essay Concerning Human Understanding,* abridged and edited by A. S. Pringle-Pattison (Oxford: Clarendon, 1924), 1.1.2.

48. At the end of his book Hamlyn explains that his use of this term, which he has used throughout the book, "is misleading in many ways"; but he does not explain why in that case he chose to use it, or why he did not choose instead to use an unmisleading term; *Theory of Knowledge,* 285.

49. Ayer says very much the same thing in *The Central Questions of Philosophy,* 1.

50. Ayer, *The Central Questions of Philosophy,* 1.

51. Ayer, *Philosophical Essays,* 245–46.

52. Chisholm, *Theory of Knowledge,* 2d ed. 1–2.

3. Epistemology, Philosophy, and the Nature of Man

1. In a succession of works, among which are *Perceiving: A Philosophical Analysis* (Ithaca: Cornell University Press, 1957); "Theory of Knowledge," in *Philosophy* (1964), reprinted in *The Foundations of Knowing* (1982) as "Theory of Knowledge in America" (circa 1930–1960); *Theory of Knowledge* (1966; 2d ed., 1977; 3d ed., 1989); and *The Foundations of Knowing* (1982). Other major papers are cited below.

2. E.g., in Keith Lehrer, ed., *Analysis and Metaphysics: Esays in Honor of R. M. Chisholm* (Dordrecht and Boston: Reidel, 1975); "Essays on the Philosophy of Roderick M. Chisholm," special number of *Grazer Philosophische Studien* 7–8 (1978), reprinted as *Essays on the Philosophy of Roderick M. Chisholm*, ed. Ernest Sosa (Amsterdam: Editions Rodopi N.V., 1979); "Papers on the Philosophy of Roderick M. Chisholm with His Replies," *Philosophia: Philosophical Quarterly of Israel* 7, nos. 3–4 (July 1978).

3. First formulated in *Theory of Knowledge* (1966); then developed, with Robert G. Keim, in "A System of Epistemic Logic," *Ratio* 14, no. 2 (December 1972): 99–115; then developed further in *Theory of Knowledge* (2d ed., 1977).

4. Chisholm, *Theory of Knowledge*, 2d ed., 12. Hereafter this edition will be cited in text.

5. That this is the case is argued in G. Chatalian, "Early Indian Buddhism and the Nature of Philosophy," *Journal of Indian Philosophy* 11 (1983):167–222, especially section 5 (201–5) and section 4 (197–209), which lays the ground for the critique advanced in section 2.1.

6. I know of no satisfactory explanation in the philosophical literature. Those of Sextus Empiricus seem better than any advanced in the twentieth century.

7. Locke, *Essay* 1.1.2.

8. Locke, *Essay*, 4.

9. Locke, *Essay*, 4.11.8.

10. Aristotle *Metaphysics*, book B (I.995ª25–27). My understanding of this passage came through the treatment of it by Giovanni Reale, *The Concept of First Philosophy and the Unity of the Metaphysics of Aristotle*, ed. and trans. John R. Catan (Albany: State University of New York Press, 1980), originally published as *Il concetto di filosofia prima a l'unità della Metafisica di Aristotele* (Milan: Vita e Pensiero, 1961; 2d ed., 1965; 3d ed., 1967). The translation is of the third edition and is authorized by the author.

11. It is perhaps clear that in advancing this view I am by implication denying the economic determinism of Karl Marx and the instrumentalism of John Dewey.

12. Aristotle *Metaphysics* Book A (I.980ª22).

13. It is perhaps worth recording the fact that I have quite unintentionally found some evidence for this generalization in conversations with illiterate persons.

14. Cf. A. J. Toynbee, *Greek Historical Thought* (New York: New American Library, Mentor, 1952), xxvii: "Thinking is as unnatural and arduous an activity for human beings as walking on two legs is for monkeys. We seldom do more of it than we have to."

15. Although I cannot and would not claim Hao Wang's endorsement of the present work—I know that he questions much of it—I think I can justifiably claim that my general philosophical outlook is very much in accord with that which he formulates in *Beyond Analytic Philosophy: Doing Justice to What We Know*. However, I would ask why philosophers cannot aspire to do justice not only to what we know, but also to what we do not yet know but only dimly sense, and even to what we do not yet know and do not yet even dimly sense—not only in metaphysics but also in epistemology and in moral philosophy. The antecedent in Strawson's "If there are no new truths to be discovered, there are old truths to be rediscovered" seems to me to be untrue in epistemology, moral philosophy, *and* metaphysics.

Name Index

Aenesidemus, 17, 19, 36
Agrippa, 17, 19, 36
Alexander the Great, 30, 35
Anaxarchus, 30
Annas, Julia, 19, 26, 29, 30, 63n.5, 65n.9, 66nn. 11, 12
Arcesilaus of Pitane, 36
Aristocles, 21, 29
Aristotle, 16, 36, 37, 41, 45–46, 54
Armstrong, David M., 60n.23
Ayer, A. J., 1, 4, 5, 6, 7, 8, 9, 10, 11, 36, 45, 46, 52, 54, 60nn. 10, 14, 15

Barnes, Jonathan, 19, 26, 29, 30, 31, 36, 63n.5, 65n.9, 66nn. 11, 12, 69nn. 34, 36, 70n.37
Bayle, Pierre, 10
Bochenski, I. J., 37
Bogomolov, A. S., 68n.18
Bolyai, J., 38
Buddha, Siddhatta Gotama the, 61–62n.32
Burnet, John, 4, 25, 26, 29, 30, 69n.34
Burnyeat, Myles, 10
Bury, R. G., 21, 66n.13
Butcharov, Panayot, 59n.7

Carnap, Rudolf, 5–6, 8, 9
Carneades, 14, 36
Chatalian, George, 71n.5
Chisholm, Roderick M., 11–12, 39, 40, 41, 42, 43, 44, 45, 46, 47–50, 54, 59n.3, 62nn. 41, 44, 64n.5, 65n.7, 66n.10
Cicero, 29, 35
Cleitomachus, 14
Collingwood, R. G., 36
Cornford, F. M., 31

Danto, Arthur C., 7, 9, 45, 46, 60n.14, 62n.39

Democritus, 13, 36
Descartes, René, 12, 13, 41, 42
Dewey, John, 71n.11
Diogenes Laertius, 29, 34–35

Eusebius, Bishop, 21

Flintoff, E., 69n.32
Forster, Michael N., 66–68n.17
Frede, Michael, 64–65n.5

Gauss, C. F., 38
Gorgias, 28–29, 32, 36, 70n.37
Grant, Alexander, 59n.7
Guthrie, W. K. C., 4, 31, 36, 37, 69n.34, 70n.39

Hahn, Hans, 4, 60n.10
Hamlyn, D. W., 2–3, 8, 9, 12, 13, 17, 19, 21, 29, 30, 31, 32, 36, 37, 40–46, 48, 50, 52, 54, 60n.10, 61n.23
Hegel, G. W. F., 21, 34, 64n.5, 66–68n.17
Heraclitus, 17, 38, 52
Hume, David, 5, 8, 10, 11, 21, 37

Kenny, Anthony, 7
Kerferd, G. B., 70n.37
Kirk, G. S., 31

Leibniz, G. W., 37
Leucippus, 13, 36
Lewis, C. I., 37
Liddell, Henry George and Scott, Robert, 69n.29
Lobachevsky, N. I., 38
Locke, John, 41, 42, 53–54
Long, A. A., 21, 25, 26, 27, 29, 30

Marx, Karl, 71n.11
Metrodorus of Chios, 13, 28, 31, 35

SUBJECT INDEX

INDEX OF GREEK TERMS, PHRASES, AND SENTENCES CITED AND/OR DISCUSSED

GEORGE CHATALIAN LAST TAUGHT AT THE UNIVERSITY OF IFE (NIGERIA) AS Visiting Professor of Philosophy (1978–83); earlier, he taught at the University of Lagos (Nigeria), where he also served as Head of the Department of Philosophy (1976–78). Since his retirement from teaching in 1983 he has devoted himself mainly to the preparation of the following book-length works: a comprehensive critical study of the worldview of a noted American philosopher recently deceased; a comprehensive critical study (in a series of works) of the philosophy of Leo Tolstoy; and an anthology of early (Indian) Buddhist Discourses (*suttas*) designed to serve as the basis of systematic philosophical study of early Indian Buddhism. His present research also includes the study of M. K. Gandhi's philosophy of nonviolent reform both in its own terms and in terms of its relation to the Tolstoyan ideas from which in part it was derived. Since 1950 he has published articles in American and African philosophical journals on probability theory, metaphysics, the nature of philosophy, global philosophy, early Indian Buddhism, and Madhyamika Buddhism.